Contemporary Crafts

Stained Glass

MARC GERSTEIN
AND LYNETTE WRIGLEY

Contemporary Crafts

Stained Glass

MARC GERSTEIN
AND LYNETTE WRIGLEY

NEW HOLLAND

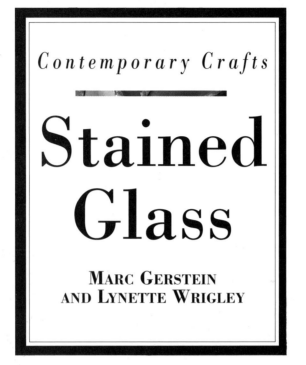

To the memory of Howard

First published in 1995 by New Holland (Publishers) Ltd
London • Cape Town • Sydney • Singapore

Reprinted 1996 and 1997

24 Nutford Place
London W1H 6DQ
United Kingdom

80 McKenzie Street
Cape Town 8001
South Africa

3/2 Aquatic Drive
Frenchs Forest, NSW 2086
Australia

ISBN 1 85368 536 4 (hbk)
ISBN 1 85368 662 X (pbk)

Editor: Coral Walker
Art director: Paul Cooper
Photographer: George Zawadzki
Illustrator: PCD

Printed and bound in Singapore by Tien Wah Press (Pte) Ltd

ACKNOWLEDGEMENTS
The authors would like to thank the staff at Lead & Light in London
for their help and support and to George Zawadzki for his patient photography.
Also to Waltham Carpets, Waltham Abbey for the kind loan of carpets.

Every effort has been made to present clear and accurate instructions.
Therefore, the authors and publishers can accept no liability for any injury,
illness or damage which may inadvertently be caused to the user
while following these instructions.

CONTENTS

INTRODUCTION

WITHIN THE LAST twenty years or so, there has been a tremendous surge of interest in glass as both an art form and a craft. For those interested in taking up glass as a hobby, there is now a wealth of knowledge and an entire industry offering materials and equipment to make glass work accessible to anyone with the desire to learn and experiment.

Learning this new skill appeals to people for many different reasons. For most, there is the pleasure in making something that is both functional and creative. In this book, we have tried to take a fresh approach to this classic craft by including a basic framework of techniques aimed at different skill levels. The projects we have selected show a variety of decorative glass work that demonstrates the wonderful versatility of glass and the stunning range of pieces you can make at home without the more specialised tools and skilful techniques employed by the professional stained glass worker.

Glass has been known and produced by man from very early times, long before the Christian era. As early as 4,000 BC, the Egyptians developed the techniques for making glass vessels, beads and glazes for pottery. But it was the Romans who appear to be the first to perfect methods of blowing glass into pieces large enough to fit into a window.

The basic ingredient of glass is, and always has been, silica, which is either sand, quartz crystals or flint. The most common glass is formed by melting silica with stabilisers and a flux at approximately 2,700 degrees fahrenheit, a temperature that could be reached in a charcoal-fired furnace. Metal oxides are added to this mixture to produce the brilliant colours that have always been associated with stained glass. Minute traces of copper or iron produce green while the addition of gold chloride was discovered to create rich rose pink tones. Even today, manufacturers of glass are constantly developing new colours or duplicating those from the past by experimenting with various combinations of oxides.

To many, stained glass is perceived as having a chiefly religious significance, and quite rightly, as this is indeed the case. In medieval times the stained glass windows of the church served as a way of instructing a largely illiterate population by illustrating the lessons from the Holy Scriptures. At this time, stained glass was an entirely religious medium found only in places of worship. Fortunately, for us today, many stunning examples of medieval glass have miraculously survived the centuries and can still be viewed in their original settings, from tiny local churches to vast, grand cathedrals.

Not until the 19th century was there a shift from using stained glass purely as a religious feature to a form of decoration that could be enjoyed in everyday, domestic buildings. The rising prosperity of Victorian Britain, combined with an unprecedented surge in building, saw

An artistic interpretation of Louis Comfort Tiffany's beautifully-detailed 'Oyster Bay' window.

A detail of an early Victorian domestic window.

stained glass become literally a household item. The studios of William Morris and Edward Burne-Jones, among others, led this transition in stained glass by offering designs that were wholly acceptable to the private home. The age of domestic stained glass had begun.

In America the introduction of domestic stained glass can almost solely be attributed to the innovation and designs of Louis Comfort Tiffany. He moved away from the old traditions of hand painting, and the heavy lead cames, used to assemble stained glass, were replaced with a new technique of wrapping glass in a thin copper foil which was then soldered together in intricate, delicate patterns. The hand cast, marble-like opal glass he developed after much experimentation still serves as a benchmark for the glass manufacturers of today. Perhaps best known for his lampshades, Tiffany offered his enthusiastic public glasswork designed around the themes of nature. A prime example of Tiffany's bold and dramatic use of colour and design are the Oyster Bay windows as portrayed in the reproduction, shown on page 7.

The ending of the Second World War saw the beginning of yet another period of change for stained glass. As many of the bomb-damaged cathedrals and public buildings in Europe were re-built, bold new panels were commissioned to replace the traditional figurative stained glass. This contemporary movement spread and was eagerly accepted by American artists working in the many new and modern buildings.

In the last twenty years, stained glass has experienced further major changes as awareness has shifted from the wonders of double glazing to the efforts required to replace or restore original glass features. It now seems a terrible waste that ageing Victorian leaded lights with layers of city grime, buckled and broken through decades of use, were hastily removed and discarded to make way for secure, thermally-correct sheets of glass.

During the early to late 1970s, collectors of stained glass could find, even on market stalls, inexpensive examples of beautifully designed and well-crafted panels from the last century. Many leaded lights were simply broken up and sold for the scrap value of the lead, as there was simply no market for 'secondhand' glazing.

However, almost overnight, this trend seemed to reverse and old front door panels with delicately painted birds or glorious stairwell windows were in great demand and purchased at ever increasing prices to be carefully restored to their original beauty.

Fortunately, so much quality stained glass was produced in both large and small studios in the 1800s, for homes, churches, large civic buildings and pubs, that a great many windows and panels still remain, even though sometimes in desperate need of attention.

Just two minutes walk from our studio is a large, old church whose graceful stone spire ascends in stark contrast to the surrounding angular low-rise housing. Many of the large voids that once contained stained glass are bricked up, while the windows that remain are coated with black grime and often broken where the wire mesh has been removed. Bomb damage from the last war has re-adjusted the foundations resulting in enormous cracks running ominously from floor to ceiling.

The minister kindly allowed us inside the old building, apologising for the state of this wonderful living relic of the past. The few stained glass windows that remained, softened by layers of weathering, glowed with the richness of jewels, appearing more like beautiful paintings than leaded lights.

Examples of stained glass, both old and new, can be spotted in numerous sites: modern shopping malls, old churches, pubs, town and city halls, cathedrals, Victorian houses, museums and restaurants. Once you take an interest in stained glass you will be delighted to find it in a variety of settings.

Most modern writers have pointed out that the mysterious charm of stained glass lies in the relationship that exists between glass and light. Glass windows or panels can look different according to the time of day, the season and the weather. The image we perceive will be affected accordingly, sometimes dramatically. Stained glass could be said to be the most ancient and cunning form of kinetic art.

Whether you are a total novice or have some experience working with glass, we hope this book will serve as an instructive and inspirational source to take you further into the realms of this fascinating art form.

ABOVE Bereft of its former glory this boarded up window reflects the state of neglect of many church windows today. RIGHT A richly coloured 19th century window from the same inner city church.

Materials and Equipment

One of the surprising aspects of learning about glass as a hobby, is how little outlay is required to get yourself started. Although there are several essential tools that are specific to glass, many of the accessories you will need can be found in the home.

A specialist stained glass supplier is your best source of materials and information. They will advise you on which tools and materials are suitable for getting your first and subsequent projects off the drawing board and into glass. Refer to page 89 for useful addresses or consult the yellow pages under 'Stained Glass' or 'Leaded Lights' for your nearest supplier. Most firms supplying materials will also offer a mail order service.

GLASS

Walking into a well-stocked coloured glass warehouse can be a bewildering experience, simply because there are so many different types and colours of glass. The coloured glass industry has exploded in the last twenty years with both new and established manufacturers offering a tremendous range of glass. Coloured or 'art glass' is produced in both Europe and the United States. As in most industries, glass manufacturers can either be small specialist firms making a limited, handmade product or large companies producing volumes of coloured glass.

Glass can be divided into two categories.

ANTIQUE GLASS: Glass that is mouth-blown by a highly skilled glass worker is known as 'Antique Glass'. The antique refers to the centuries-old technique of producing glass by blowing a cylinder or a 'muffle' which is re-heated and flattened into workable sheets. Antique glass is known for its brilliant surface qualities, clarity and range of colour. Each sheet is unique, having its own particular irregularities and qualities. This glass is labour intensive to make and is usually more than double the cost of a similar coloured glass made by machine. The best known producers of antique or mouth-blown glass are located in Europe.

ROLLED GLASS: The second type of glass is 'Rolled Glass', which is generally a machine-made product that is rolled out in a hot, near liquid, state on to a metal surface. Within this category of glass are two general types that are easily identifiable. **Opal glass** is not transparent and is ideal for transmitting artificial electric light. **Cathedral glass** is generally transparent and used in natural light situations. The USA is the source of most rolled cathedral and opal glass manufactured today.

When you visit your supplier to select glass,

TOP RIGHT *Antique glass*
RIGHT *Opal glass (Opalescent)*

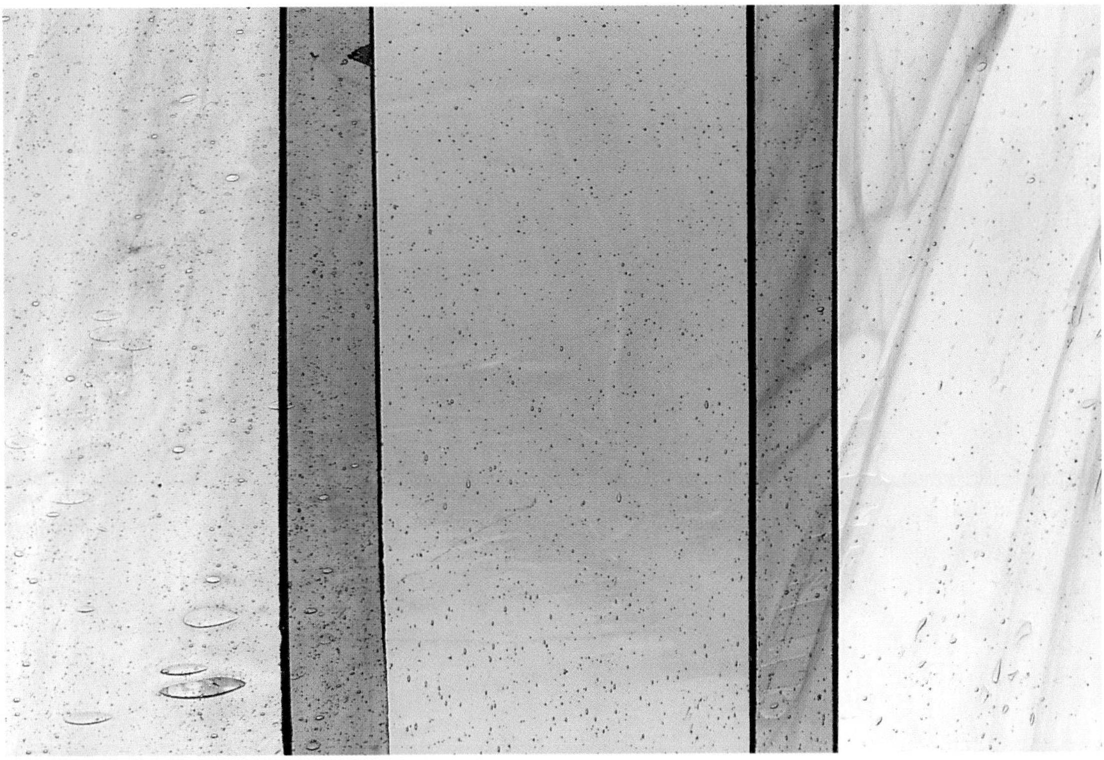

take along a drawing of your project. A good supplier will take you through the various glasses on display and help you select the appropriate glass in terms of cost and colour. Hold the pieces up to the light or use a lightbox when selecting colours. In order to know what to ask for when

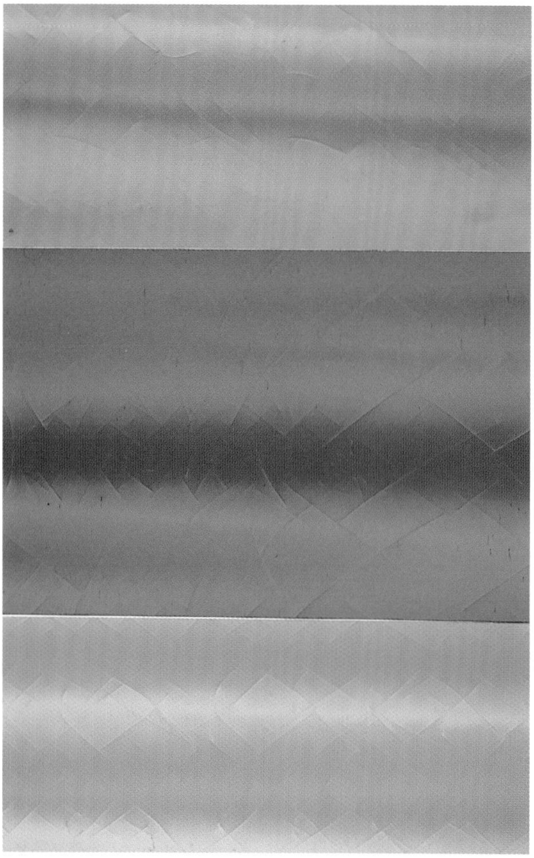

visiting a supplier, we have listed and explained some of the glass you will encounter.

Streaky glass Any glass with two or more colours swirled together.

Seedy glass Air bubbles are allowed to form within this clear or tinted glass. Often used as a background glass.

Semi-antique A machine-made glass similar in appearance to mouth-blown but without the variation.

Iridised glass This has a surface appearance similar to oil on water and is available on most types of rolled glasses.

Hand-rolled glass A more expensive and expressive glass usually associated with the work of Tiffany.

TOP *Machine-made patterned glass* LEFT *Semi-antique* BELOW *Hand-rolled*

GLASS CUTTERS

The main skill for working with glass is the technique of cutting. All glass cutters are basically pencil-shaped tools with a hardened steel wheel for scoring the surface of the glass. The metal ball at one end is used to 'tap' a score, causing the glass to fracture and break apart. Most people find cutting the most satisfying and challenging aspect of creative glass work.

The type or quality of the cutting wheel divides glass cutters into three groups.

STEEL WHEEL CUTTERS The least expensive cutter has a steel cutting wheel which will wear rather quickly. This cutter is perhaps best used as a beginner's tool that can be discarded quickly as you progress.

CARBIDE STEEL WHEEL CUTTERS Cutters with this hard wheel are more expensive but will last longer. Easy to use, the cutter requires less pressure and is the type we have used in the projects in this book.

TUNGSTEN CARBIDE WHEEL CUTTERS These type of cutters often have a built-in oil reservoir and are noted for their long life and comfort to hold. The diameter of the wheel is smaller than other types of cutters, allowing for greater control when cutting intricate shapes.

CUTTING OIL To prolong the life of a cutter and improve your score, keep a jar with cotton wool soaked in a mixture of white spirit and light machine oil.

CUTTING SURFACE

Thin carpet, felt or cork placed on a waist-high table are all good surfaces to use for cutting glass. Keep a dustpan and brush handy to remove tiny glass slivers.

PLIERS

There are basically two types specifically designed for stained glass work.

GROZING/BREAKER PLIERS These are used to remove small irregular sections of glass accurately. They differ from conventional pliers by having curved serrated jaws designed for gripping the glass.

RUNNING PLIERS These plastic or metal pliers are designed for breaking long, thin glass cuts.

CUTTING SET SQUARE

Use this for squaring off glass. A lip on the lower edge ensures a perfect right angle.

CARBORUNDUM STONE

This natural stone files away sharp glass edges especially prior to copper foiling.

ELECTRIC GLASS GRINDERS Expensive, but helpful, machines to achieve dramatic edge control. An electric, water cooled grinder is the tool many serious glass workers aspire to own.

SOLDERING

Soldering is the technique of joining two sections of metal together by melting solder where they meet. This is necessary for lead and copper foil work.

SOLDERING IRON For glass work you will need a soldering iron with a minimum output of 75 watts fitted with a plated, screwdriver-shaped tip. Small soldering irons used for electrical repairs are not up to the task of melting the amount of solder required for glass work. Most irons will reach their working temperature in 4-5 minutes. Irons are available with a built-in temperature control unit that are a pleasure to use but expensive to buy.

IRON STAND A wise place for a hot iron.

SOLDER An alloy or combination of tin and lead. We use 50/50 (tin/solder) in the projects that follow. Solder with a higher tin content is available and this will have a lower melting point and flow easier giving a more silver-like finish. Solder is available either by the length or in 500 g (1 lb) rolls.

FLUX A liquid, paste or solid substance used when soldering which allows the solder to flow when melted with the iron. Use a **non-toxic liquid** for soldering on copper foil and **tallow flux** for soldering lead cames.

TIP CLEANER A specialised sponge or chemical used to remove deposits that will accumulate on soldering iron tips. A clean tip will transfer heat efficiently to the work.

COPPER FOIL

A copper tape with an adhesive backing is used to wrap around each piece of glass before soldering the pieces together. Available in various widths suitable for all types of colour glass, copper foil offers a strong, versatile method of assembly.

Foil is available in different widths to accommodate the thickness of the glass. As it is made in the United States of America, foil tape comes in imperial sizes. Either 7/32 in (5 mm) or ¼ in (6 mm) foil is suitable for 2.5 – 3 mm (⅛ in) coloured glass used in all the projects.

PATINA FOR COPPER FOIL Used to change the colour of solder from silver to either black or a copper colour.

FID A pencil-type implement used to smooth down the edges of glass wrapped with copper foil and open the channels of lead cames.

LEAD WORK

There are a number of materials and equipment used specifically in lead work.

LEAD CAMES

The term 'leaded lights' couldn't be more appropriate when describing a stained glass window. Strips of H-section lead – called cames – have channels either side and are used to hold the glass in place, before being soldered at the joints. Cames are available in many widths and profiles. For the projects we use 6 mm (¼ in) round for the internal leading and 12 mm (½ in) flat around the perimeter.

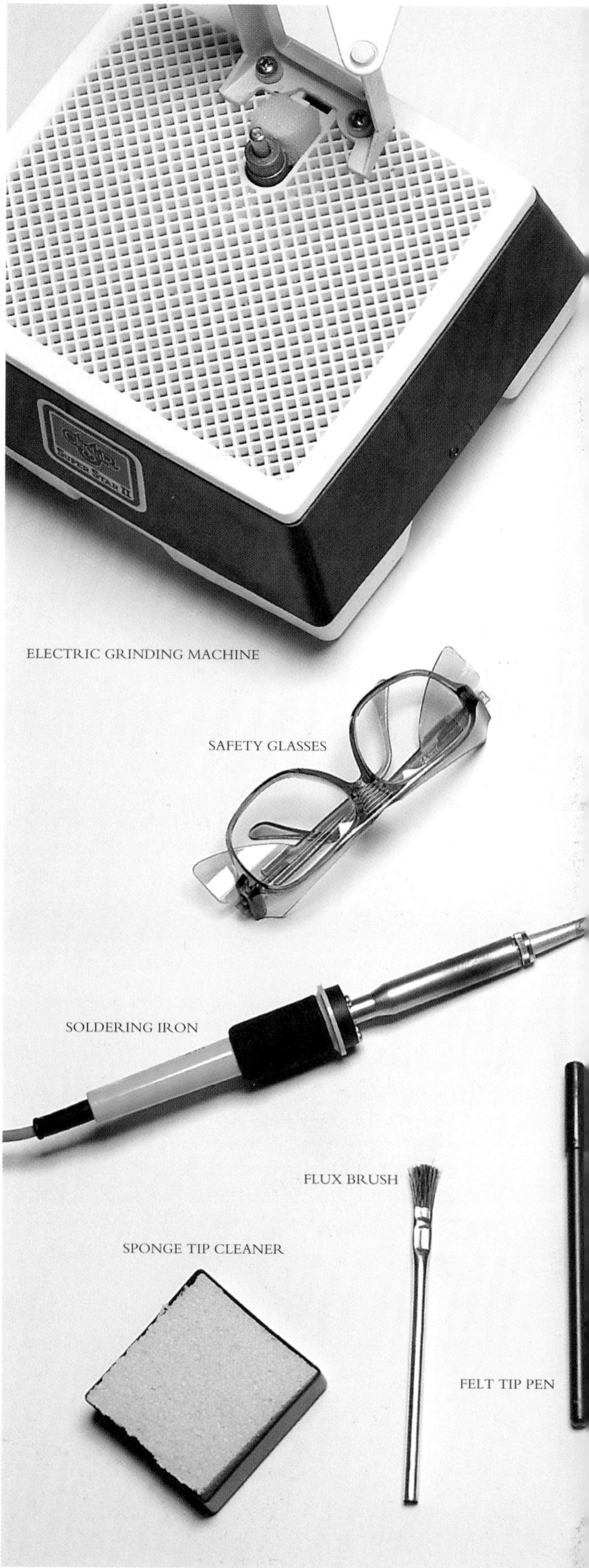

RUNNING PLIERS
LEAD KNIFE
LEAD VICE
CUTTING OIL JAR
GROZING PLIERS
CEMENT BRUSH
SNIPS
FID
CARBORUNDUM STONE
CARBIDE CUTTER
OIL CUTTERS
SOLDERING IRON REST
CIRCLE CUTTER
CUTTING SQUARE

LEAD VICE
Lead cames are stretched just prior to use to both straighten and increase their strength.

LEAD KNIFE
A knife with a sharp, curved blade especially adapted for cutting cames cleanly. Often supplied with a weighted handle which is used for tapping nails.

HORSE SHOE NAILS
Ideal for holding pieces of glass in position before soldering.

LEAD LIGHT CEMENT
A specialised putty that finishes and weather-proofs a leaded panel. Use a nail brush or something similar to apply the cement. Whiting (a chalk-like absorbent powder) is used for final cleaning of the leaded light.

OTHER MATERIALS

GLASS GLUE A transparent glue for adhering glass to glass. (For the Glass Gem Mirror on page 48 we have used clear bath sealant which isn't actually a glue but gives excellent results.)

ETCHING CREAM: Glass can be worked in a number of ways. It can be abraded with a fine jet of pressurised sand (sand-blasting) or etched with hydrofluoric acid to create detailed, delicate designs. These two techniques are used by professional glass workers and have developed into recognised specialities requiring a considerable amount of expertise and equipment. There is, however, an alternative available to individuals who want to decorate glass in a similar manner but who do not have access to the facilities for sand-blasting or acid etching. Using a proprietary etching cream is a very straightforward process that will create a light, frosted surface when applied to glass. Used with care, it produces a delicate, frosted image on the glass surface with little more than a paintbrush, plastic bowl and access to running water. This method was used to create the Fish Bowl and Frosted Vase on pages 36 and 78.

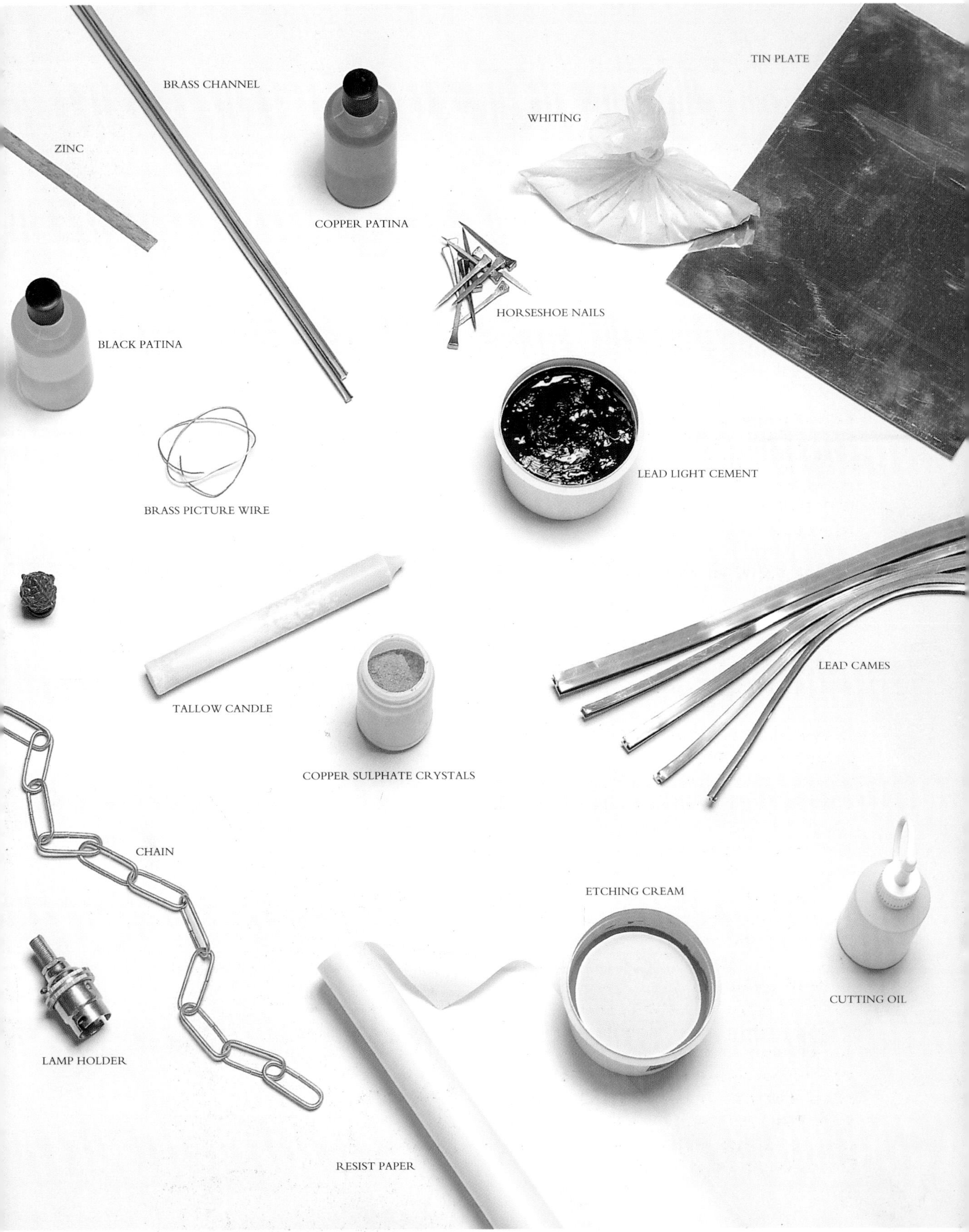
TIN PLATE
BRASS CHANNEL
WHITING
ZINC
COPPER PATINA
HORSESHOE NAILS
BLACK PATINA
LEAD LIGHT CEMENT
BRASS PICTURE WIRE
LEAD CAMES
TALLOW CANDLE
COPPER SULPHATE CRYSTALS
CHAIN
ETCHING CREAM
CUTTING OIL
LAMP HOLDER
RESIST PAPER

Basic Techniques

LEARNING TO CUT GLASS

It's fascinating to watch an experienced glass cutter effortlessly scoring and breaking glass. Glass cutting is all about confidence and practise and is a skill that can be learned by almost anyone who can hold a pencil. Most glaziers will have plenty of 2-3 mm (⅛ in) clear glass off-cuts perfect for practice and learning how to control a glass cutter.

HOLDING THE GLASS CUTTER

Hold the cutter firmly. There are a few ways of holding a cutter depending upon both the type of cutter and the way you find most comfortable. You must be able to see the cutting wheel and apply pressure as you steer the cutter over the smooth side of the glass.

SCORING THE GLASS

Practice cutting by making random scores on scrap glass, applying a consistent pressure. The centre of the cutting wheel should be at a right angle to the glass surface. A good score is both seen and heard. The cutter will make an audible noise if you apply enough pressure. Release this pressure just 1 mm (a fraction of an inch) before you reach the glass edge. Never go over the score line a second time. This will ruin a cutting wheel and not improve your score. Make adjustments to your grip as you practice scoring. As you will often be following the lines of your design, you should be pushing the cutter forwards – away from your body – to effectively see where you are going.

USING THE CUTTING SQUARE

When you need to cut a straight line, use the cutting square. Place the cutter next to the edge of the square with the cutter firmly on the glass. Pull the glass cutter towards the body and keep an even pressure down on the glass ensuring the square is steady.

Score straight lines by using the cutting square. Hold the ruler down firmly while pressing and pulling the cutter confidently towards the body.

BREAKING THE SCORE

How well you have scored the glass will become apparent as the breaking process begins. A well-scored piece of glass will break with very little effort. Scored glass should be broken or snapped while the score is still new.

The best way to begin building up your cutting confidence is to use your bare hands as a breaking tool. Hold the scored piece of glass firmly with the thumb on either side of the scored line. Place your index fingers underneath

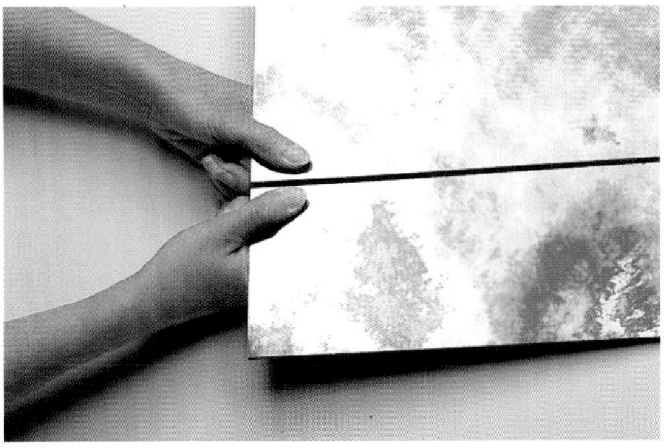

Break the glass by holding it close to the scored line and snapping it apart with your hands.

and snap the glass sharply up and outwards causing the glass to separate.

Long straight scores can also be snapped off by using the edge of your work table. Place the glass with scored side facing up on the exact edge of the table. Raise the piece to an angle of 45 degrees and bring it down smartly on the table edge to cause a break.

Tips: Always work with a piece of glass that is not too much bigger than the shape you want to cut. Always start a score from the edge of the glass and continue it to another edge. A score that stops in the middle of a piece of glass will end up breaking just where it pleases and not where you would like it to.

TAPPING

Glass has a tendency to break in straight lines but fortunately there are a number of ways of convincing the break to follow a curve. Most glass cutters have a metal ball at one end; this is used for tapping underneath a score causing it to fracture and break. See this for yourself by scoring a piece of window glass and tapping the underneath of the score. You will notice how the score changes in appearance as the tapping causes a fracture along the score.

USING THE GROZER/RUNNING PLIERS

Where you are not able to use your hands to break apart two pieces of glass, try the help of the pliers. Hold the glass with one hand and with the other place the straight jaw edge of the pliers next to the score. Holding the glass and the pliers firmly, grip the glass and make a sharp downward movement with the wrist. The glass should snap apart. Any small unwanted chips of glass left on the edges can be nipped off using the pliers in the same way.

GROZING Hold the glass firmly with one hand and gently roll the pliers backwards to take off small sections of glass with the serrated inside surface of the jaws. Glass chips will fly when grozing and we recommend you wear a pair of safety glasses.

RUNNING PLIERS These are used to break long, narrow pieces of glass. A mark on the top of the jaws is lined up with the glass score. Gently squeeze the pliers which will cause the score to run and separate.

GRINDING AND POLISHING

Well-cut glass only needs to be rubbed gently along its edges with a carborundum stone to remove any sharp protrusions. Keep the stone wet to prevent glass dust forming as you rub the edges on the abrasive surface.

Glass can also be polished using wet and dry abrasive paper. Polish the glass edge by rubbing with wet fine grade paper. This method is used

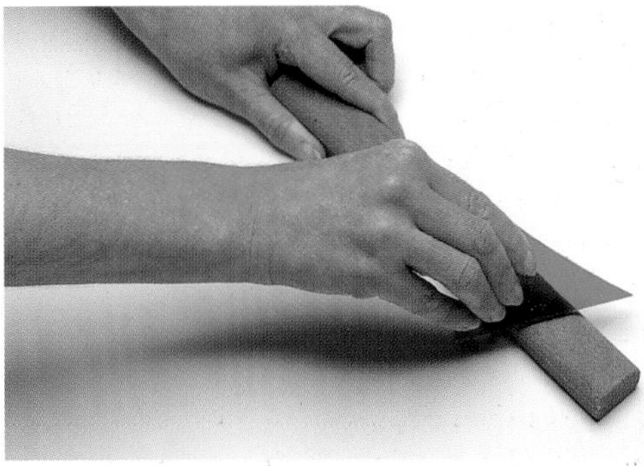

Rub the edges of the glass back and forth over the stone to remove sharp slivers.

to make any exposed glass edge safe to handle.

For a really professional finish, you might like to try an electric glass grinder. Push the glass against the spinning diamond-impregnated wheel. Keep your eye on the water level, frequently checking the glass against the pattern. If the machine is not fitted with an eye shield it is advisable to wear safety glasses.

CONVEX CURVES After scoring a curve you will find it easier to break if you then make a series of short tangent scores off the main score.

A series of scores running to the edges of the glass will enable the glass to be tapped out.

Alternatively many short scores can be made around a circle or small roundish shape and then broken off by tapping and using the grozer/breaker pliers.

COPPER FOIL

This technique enables glass to be assembled into a pattern or design without the use of lead to hold it together. Instead, a narrow copper foil tape is applied to the edges of cut pieces of glass. The foil on two adjoining pieces of glass is then soldered together.

After wrapping the edges of the glass with foil and folding over the sides, smooth the foil down with a fid or other plastic tool.

APPLYING COPPER FOIL

Glass that has been cut, washed and dried is ready for wrapping. Always overlap the tape by 6 mm (¼ in) on each edge of the glass, using care to centre the foil on the glass edge. The foiled edges must be smoothed or 'crimped' after wrapping to create neat, smooth seams. Use a fid to do this (see above).

SOLDERING

Allow the iron to reach working temperature and wipe the tip clean with a sponge or tip cleaner. Coat the hot tip with a small amount of solder. The iron is now 'tinned' with easily melting solder and ready for work.

There are three soldering skills to learn when working with copper foil. Foil up some scrap pieces of glass and experiment with each of the three soldering steps. Flux allows the solder to flow and must always be applied with a brush to the copper foiled area before soldering.

1 TACKING To prevent movement once a foiled piece of glass is positioned. Brush on flux and spot or tack solder in several places. Use a small amount of solder.

2 TINNING All edges wrapped with foil must be soldered with a thin coat of solder. On the inside seams brush on flux and tin with a hot iron.

Tack the positioned pieces together by applying a small drop of solder. Always brush some flux on the area to be soldered first.

Move the iron steadily across the seam applying solder sparingly.

3 BEAD OR 'FINISH' SOLDERING This is applied to all exterior seams that are visible and is the soldering technique that requires the most practice. Brush flux on to the copper foil and slowly move the iron along the seam, feeding the tip with solder. The solder will melt and a dome shaped, smooth soldered seam can be achieved with practice. Keep your tip clean by wiping it on a damp sponge whenever deposits

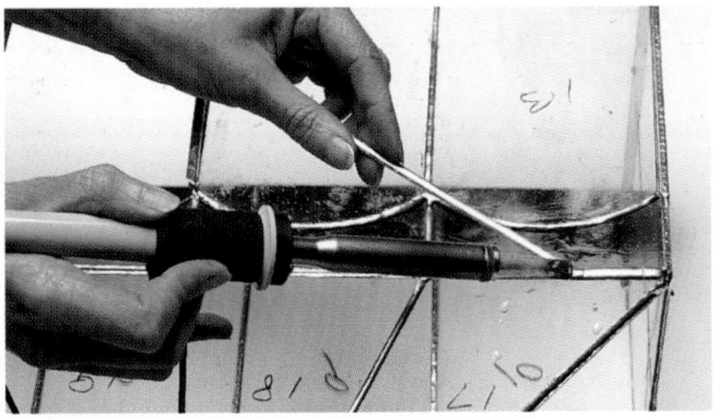

Apply enough solder to form a 'bead' for a smooth finish to the seams. Hold the iron with a steady hand and allow enough solder to melt while moving slowly along the seam.

form. Remember to re-flux the seam each time you repeat 'finish' soldering. When you are satisfied with your soldering turn the project over and tin solder the inside seam.

FINISHING COPPER FOIL PROJECTS

Flux is mildly corrosive and projects will have a much better finish if washed off with warm, soapy water when soldering is complete.

You apply patina (see page 14) with a sponge or small brush to all soldered areas, wearing rubber gloves as you work. Wash again with warm soapy water after patina has been applied.

Dry and buff with metal polish and a soft cloth for a high lustre finish.

LEADED LIGHTS

If you look at the profile of a lead came you will notice it has a centre width or 'heart' section. When drawing out your pattern for cutting glass, you must allow for this thickness, which for most lead cames is 2 mm (1/16 in). There are felt tip pens available with this same line thickness and these are ideal for drawing your pattern.

When working out a design for a leaded project, avoid any very small shaped pieces of glass. The working drawing you will make is called a cartoon. Choose a strong paper and make two copies. The perimeter of your cartoon is also the exterior edge of the border of 12 mm (½ in) flat lead. Draw another line on the inside of the perimeter, taking into account the heart or thickness of the lead. This is your actual cut line. The outside leaf of the came will remain empty and can be trimmed to fit the panel into a window frame. It is also used to hold the panel in a wooden frame with small tacks.

Draw the chosen design and trace over the lines with a felt tip pen as described above. Each piece of glass must be accurate and the exact size required. When you have finished cutting, lay the glass on the cartoon and you should have a space between each piece of glass allowing for the heart of the lead.

Make a frame to work within by placing two strips of wood at right angles and nailing them to a board or work surface with the cartoon underneath. These strips of wood should be lying flush alongside the outside perimeter of the cartoon.

STRETCHING THE LEAD

Stretch a piece of 12 mm (½ in) lead using the lead vice to grip one end while holding the other with pliers and tugging until the lead is straight.

CUTTING THE LEAD

Cut lead with the curve-shaped lead knife. Place the knife on the top of the channel and rock it gently from side to side while gently pressing down. Too much pressure or a dull knife will distort or crush the channel. It is advisable to practise cutting on scraps of lead.

First mark the length of lead required and use the lead knife to cut through the came.

OPENING THE CHANNEL

No matter how cleanly the lead is cut, some distortion is inevitable. Use the lead fid to open the channel.

LEADING THE PANEL

Cut two lengths of lead to the required size and place these on the cartoon along the wood strips. Tack two horseshoe nails at both ends of the came to hold it in place.

Working from the inside in the right angle, begin placing the glass on the cartoon, pushing it inside the channel. Generally, 6 mm (¼ in) lead is used for the inside of the panel. Remember always to stretch the lead before you continue to cut sections for placing between each piece of glass. Measure each piece of lead before you cut it and remember to make an allowance for where the next piece of lead will butt up.

As you work, hold the glass in place with horseshoe nails. Use a small piece of scrap lead in between the glass and horseshoe nail. Any adjustments to the shapes of your glass can be made along the way or re-cut using the spare

A handy horseshoe nail holds the project in place while the panel is being made. Always use a scrap piece of lead inbetween to protect the glass or lead you are holding.

cartoon as a guide. Use the pattern as a map to guide and adjust you in leading the pieces of the panel together.

When the panel is complete and you have placed the 12 mm (½ in) lead on the outside edges, tap in more horseshoe nails to hold it in place before soldering together. If there are any spaces between the end of one piece of lead and an intersecting piece, they need to be bridged together by cutting small scraps of lead which are then pushed into the gap.

It is necessary to flux each joint or intersection before you solder. Rub each joint with tallow flux (see page 14). Hold a piece of solder over each joint and allow the flat edge of the iron to melt a flat blob of solder on to the joint. Remove the iron immediately as the heat can melt the lead came.

After soldering all the joints, remove the nails, turn the panel over and, after filling in any gaps, flux and solder the joints on the other side.

CEMENTING

Leaded lights must be cemented for both strength and weather proofing. This process cleans the glass, darkens the cames and greatly improves the appearance of the finished piece.

Using a small scrubbing brush, rub the cement over the panel, taking great care to push the cement under the cames and into all the intersections. Turn the panel over and repeat the process.

Sprinkle a handful of whiting over the panel and rub all over the surface on both sides. 'Draw' around all the cames with the tip of the lead fid to remove excess cement. Sprinkle with a little more whiting and scrub the panel with a clean brush. (The whiting will help to remove grease from the glass.) The longer you scrub the glass, the darker the cames will become. The fid can be used again to remove any more cement that has leaked out from under the cames. Repeat the whole process on the other side of the panel.

ETCHING CREAM

This has been explained in detail in the Fish Bowl (page 36) and the Frosted Vase (page 78). Also, instructions will vary from manufacturer to manufacturer depending upon the strength and type of cream. Cream intended for home use contains no hydrofluoric acid and is safe to use when the manufacturer's instructions are followed.

Where the cream is applied, the glass will frost. The areas protected or masked off from the cream will remain clear or 'frost free'. You can either mask the background and frost the image as in the Fish Bowl, or work in reverse and mask the image and frost the background as in the Frosted Vase.

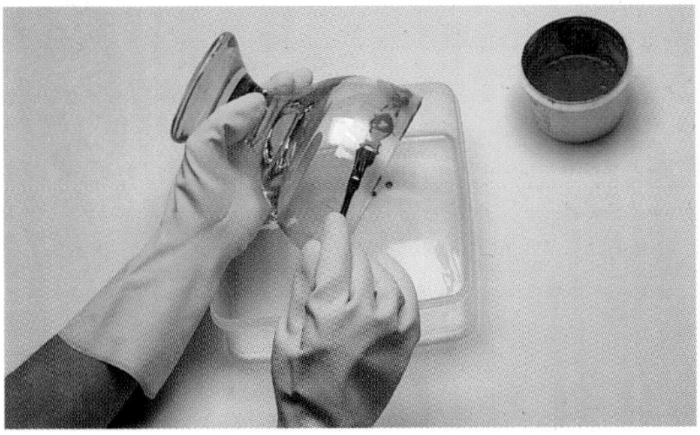

Etching paste is applied with a brush to frost the image.

Mask off the area with sticky back vinyl or, in the case of the Frosted Vase, use ordinary wood glue as the mask itself. Once your mask has dried, put on rubber gloves before mixing the cream with a plastic or wooden stick.

Work in a large plastic bowl to protect the work surface from cream as you generously brush it on the glass. How long the cream remains on the glass will depend upon the strength and type of cream. However, after approximately 15 minutes, wash off the cream with cold running water to check the results. Re-apply cream to the entire piece if some areas are not frosted to your satisfaction. After waiting another 15 minutes, repeat this procedure, washing, this time, with warm water to remove all traces of cream and to help ease the removal of the stencil.

SAFETY

Commonsense and some very basic precautions are all that are required to work safely with glass. Keep your work area tidy. Glass not in use should be stacked or boxed away. Brush the work surface frequently to remove the tiny glass slivers and check large pieces for runs or cracks before handling. We recommend wearing safety glasses when cutting or shaping glass.

Chemicals used for finishing and soldering can be harmful and should be capped and put safely away when not in use. Always wear rubber gloves and wash hands thoroughly after use.

Solder in a well ventilated area which, if possible, has an extractor fan to remove fumes. Always use a metal stand for your hot iron and remember to keep tools and materials well out of the reach from small children.

(Small cuts and nicks are inevitable from time to time. Keep some sticking plasters and antiseptic handy!)

GALLERY

THE FOLLOWING PAGES exhibit various pieces from professional artists and designers who work in stained glass today. The works range from highly-skilled reproductions of early stained glass to bold, contemporary pieces where glass and light are used to maximum effect to create exciting new images and designs. Although these works often involve skills outside the range of this book, they are presented to inspire and encourage the reader to explore the spectacular beauty of glass and the infinite possibilities of pattern and form.

~

Fused Glass Panels
JAMES PREECE
An imaginative, autonomous panel made by stacking pieces of glass in a kiln and fusing or melting them together at high temperature.

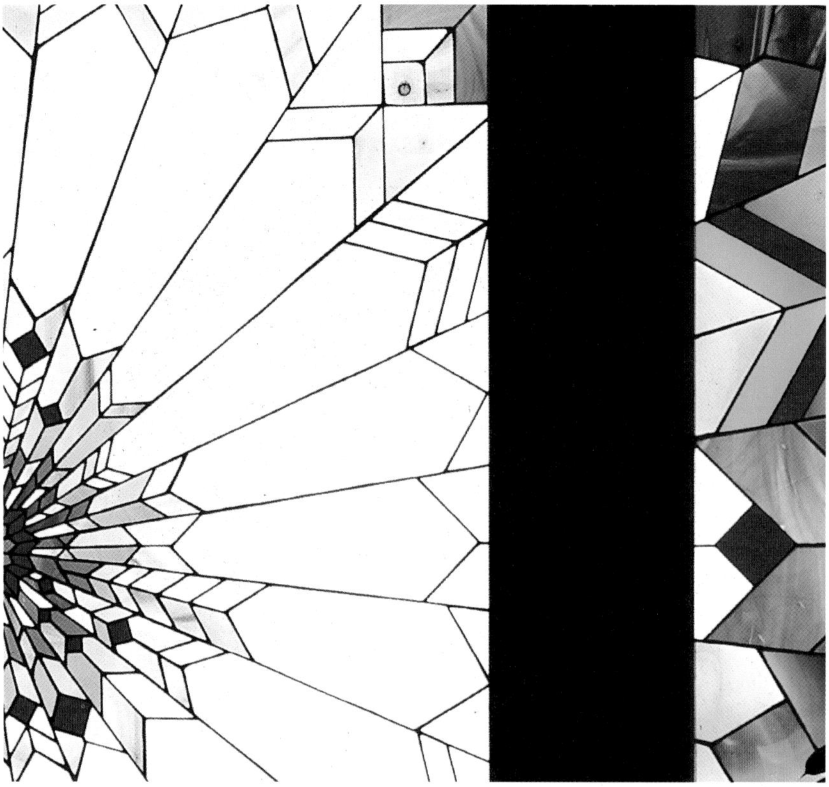

Entrance Doors
RICHARD SCOWEN
120 x 144 cm (48 x 56 in) each door.
This detail is taken from door and side panels designed and fabricated to inspire glass workers arriving at the Lead & Light studios in London. The large copper foiled panels are laminated on 6 mm (¼ in) clear glass for added strength and weatherproofing. The windows are made with full antique glass produced by Hartley Wood, the only coloured glass manufacturers in England.

. . . .

Glassworks
ANN LAMOT
A selection of drinking glasses, vases and candleholders.
Taking her inspiration from the beauty and culture of Wales, where she lives and works, the artist's pieces are designed and made using recycled bottle glass and glass gemstones.

. . . .

Lillington

RHIANNON MORGAN

Named after the client from whom it was commissioned, this window is clearly influenced by the work of early modernist painters. Either clear antique glass has been stained, or glass in a mix of primary colours has been heavily etched to produce a variety of elemental shapes. Lead lines, both real and fake, add energy and surprise to the design.

....

Child's Door Panel

90 x 20 cm (36 x 8 in)
A drawing taken, literally, from an 8-year-old artist and fabricated into two panels for the entrance doors to the child's room.

....

Bakery Window

LEAD & LIGHT

122 x 102 cm (48 x 40 in) This large copper foil panel was designed by the company Design House and fabricated by Lead & Light for a large bakery company in Britain. The fine details are painted on to the glass. The window reflects a commercial bakery's historic ties with a rural environment.

Mackerel

RHIANNON MORGAN

In this screen, the lead lines blend, almost imperceptibly into the design itself. This gives the finished piece a dynamism that paint and lustre alone could not have achieved. The mackerel are suspended in an abstract pattern of fish scales and bubbles.

Literature and Sculpture
WILLIAM LOWE
130 x 43 cm (52 x 17 in) each window.
These two windows in the pre-Raphaelite style are deliberately 'antiqued' to replicate the originals. Carefully researched by the artist and, using the same techniques and materials as the originals, these windows are a near perfect reproduction. William Lowe is a former head of the stained glass department at the Victoria and Albert Museum in London.

Synagogue Windows
JUDITH SOVIN
132 x 58 cm (53 x 23 in) each window.
The bold use of colour and upwardly flowing, lead lines are used to suggest different aspects of Judaism. These are just two of sixteen leaded windows – the Shofar (ram's horn) (left) and the memorial window which shows six stars representing the six million who died in the Holocaust.

Horses
LYNETTE WRIGLEY
3 x 1.5 m (9 x 5 ft)
A figurative window in four panels specially commissioned to grace the home of racehorse owners. This is a fine example of the detail and lifelike forms that can be achieved with the copper foil technique, without any recourse to painting.

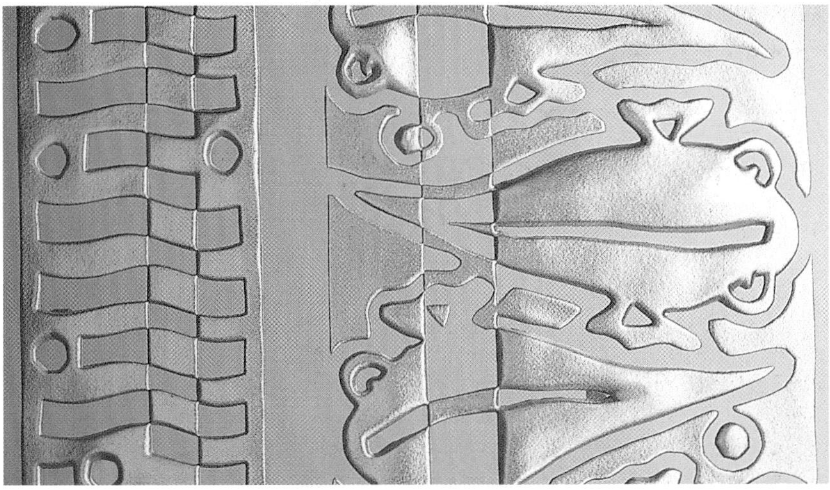

Fish Bowl *(detail)*
RHIANNON MORGAN
Here, light and glass come together to produce a dramatic, crisply executed motif which has been deeply sand-blasted. The two-dimensional effect evokes the sparkling, translucent qualities of water.

LAMPSHADE

LYNETTE WRIGLEY

THERE HAS BEEN NO SINGLE greater influence to the way people experience decorative glass than the work of Lewis Comfort Tiffany, the innovative American glass artist of the last century. With his delicate and new approach to design and fabrication, he removed decorative glass from the lofty, serious, religious environment and into private homes. His use of copper foil rather than the traditional lead cames allowed for entire new areas of glass work to be explored. Tiffany's work was characterized by intricate detail, outstanding craftmanship and an exquisite use of natural design and colour.

The many lampshades produced by the Tiffany studio were the artist's most visible contribution to the change in direction of decorative glass. This lampshade uses the copper foil technique but has a more contemporary, geometric design.

~

MATERIALS AND EQUIPMENT

• 60 cm² (2 sq ft) light amber opal glass • 23 cm (¾ sq ft) dark green opal glass • 10 cm² (4 sq in) black opal glass • 15 cm² (½ sq ft) white opal glass • 4 cm (1 ½ in) square vase cap • 7/32 in copper foil • 0.5 kg (1 lb) solder • patina • paper • felt tip pen • carbide glass cutter • running pliers • carborundum stone • soldering iron • fid • bulb holder with 2.5 cm (1 in) threaded loop • flux

1 Using the illustration and dimensions on page 86, draw up a full size pattern for one complete panel. (This is a four sided shade; each side is identical.) With the help of the cutting square begin scoring the long narrow strips, taking measurements from your pattern.

2 Use the running pliers to cut these narrow pieces. There is a raised section in the centre of the jaws of the pliers which must be placed under the scored line. Hold the glass firmly in one hand while gently squeezing the pliers; these will break the scored line. Cut all pieces four times (for the four sides) and check that they fit correctly on the pattern. Smooth the edges with a carborundum stone, wash and foil each piece. (See page 20 for more details.) Place two straight edges on either side to help you achieve a straight line. Now tack solder the foiled pieces together before beading the front and tinning the back of each panel.

3 Using a right angle board, place two panels together edge to edge and tack solder the top, centre and bottom. Repeat this step with the remaining two panels and tack solder the two halves together.

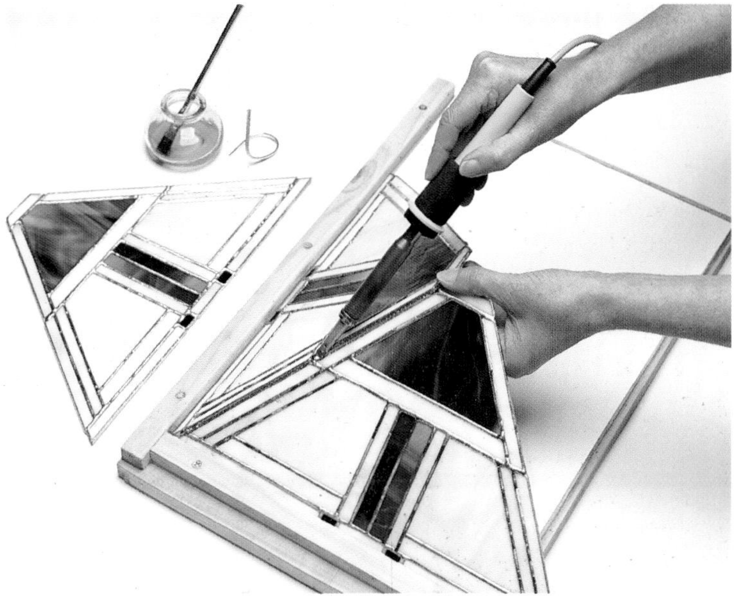

4 Solder the vase cap into position before tin soldering the exterior corner seams.

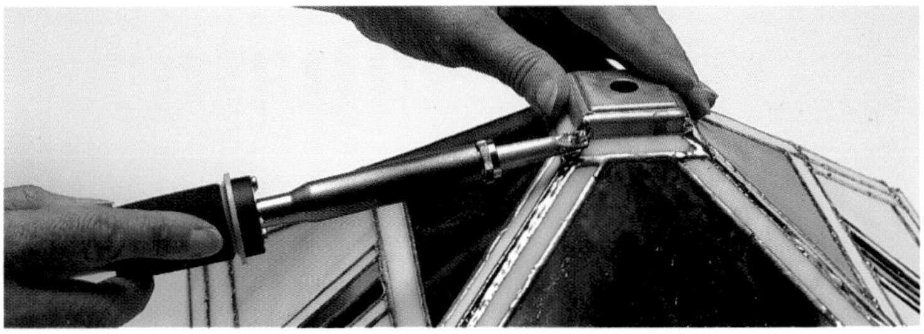

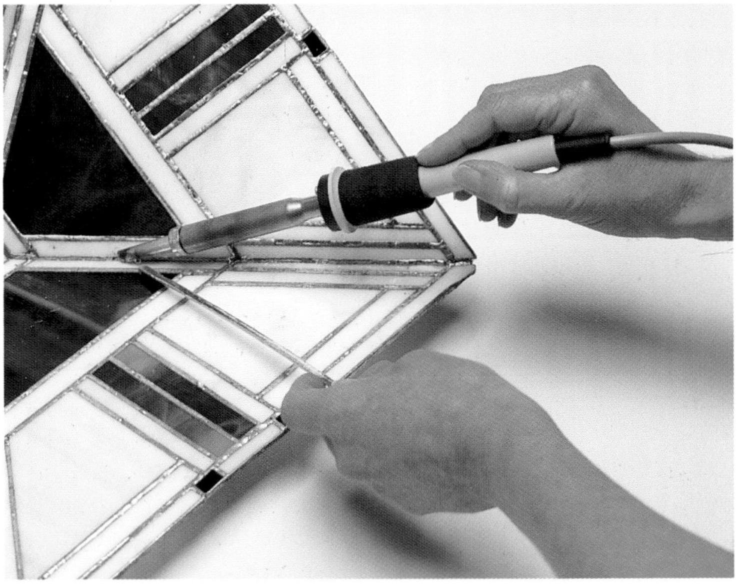

5 Turn the lamp on its side and tin solder the inside seams. Spend a few minutes bead soldering the outside corner seams for a neat, finished appearance.

6 Apply the patina and wash the shade before threading through the bulb holder.

Fish Bowl

MARC GERSTEIN

Decorate a plain glass bowl with a band of frosted fishes by using a hand-cut stencil and a proprietary etching cream. With these simple materials you can successfully create frosted glass which closely resembles professional sand-blasting.

Drinking glasses, vases, window panes or any other plain glass objects can be personalized with this technique. Start off with simple shapes that are cut easily with a scalpel or craft knife, and progress to more detailed patterns as your experience grows.

~

MATERIALS AND EQUIPMENT

• plain clear glass bowl • self-adhesive vinyl for stencil • fine felt tip pen • scalpel or craft knife • plastic bowl • rubber gloves • small paintbrush • etching cream (see page 89 for suppliers)

1 Cut the vinyl into sections that will follow the shape of the curve and overlap where necessary. The stencil should cover and mask the top of the bowl and at least 12 mm (½ in) below the image. Be sure to squeeze out any air bubbles, as these could allow the etching cream to leak under the stencil and distort the image.

2 Using a fine felt tip pen, begin to draw the image on the vinyl. You may find it helpful to place a drawing of the image on paper behind the glass first for tracing over with the pen.

3 Using a thin bladed, sharp scalpel, cut and remove all areas from the vinyl that are to be painted with the etching cream. Be sure to smooth all the edges with a cloth to prevent leakage.

4 Turn the bowl over to prevent the cream from running into areas not covered with vinyl, and begin to brush on the etching cream. Be sure to wear rubber gloves and work over a plastic bowl. The amount of time the cream must remain on the glass will depend upon its strength. You are advised to consult the manufacturer's instructions for the recommended duration. Wash off the cream under running water, remove the stencil and allow the bowl to dry.

WINDOW PANEL

LYNETTE WRIGLEY

DON'T ASSUME that a stained glass panel needs to be fixed forevermore into a window frame. Although ideal for a small window, it could also be interpreted as a glass picture that can be framed and displayed in daylight. Consider where you would like to display your panel when selecting the glass to take advantage of the the extraordinary range of colour, texture and patterns available.

The swirling, moving surface of the background glass in the copper foil panel shown here will filter out a view you would rather not see, but it will not block out the daylight. Instead, when the sun shines, you will have the pleasure of witnessing a dazzling and ever-changing pattern of colour reflected on adjacent walls and furniture.

~

MATERIALS AND EQUIPMENT

• 60 cm² (2 sq ft) clear reamy glass • 8 cm² (¼ sq ft) pink water glass • 8 cm² (¼ sq ft) antique deep pink glass • 8 cm² (¼ sq ft) antique dark green glass • 8 cm² (¼ sq ft) antique dark blue glass • 8 cm² (¼ sq ft) amber light antique glass • 4 small glass gems • 5 mm (¼ in) black backed foil • 1 kg (2 lb) solder • soldering iron • liquid flux • patina • paper • felt tip pen • carbide glass cutter • grozing pliers • electric sander or carborundum stone

1 Draw two full size patterns from the one shown on page 86; one to cut from and one to lay the finished pieces on. The glass used in this project is transparent so it is possible to lay the chosen colours over the pattern and score directly over the design lines.

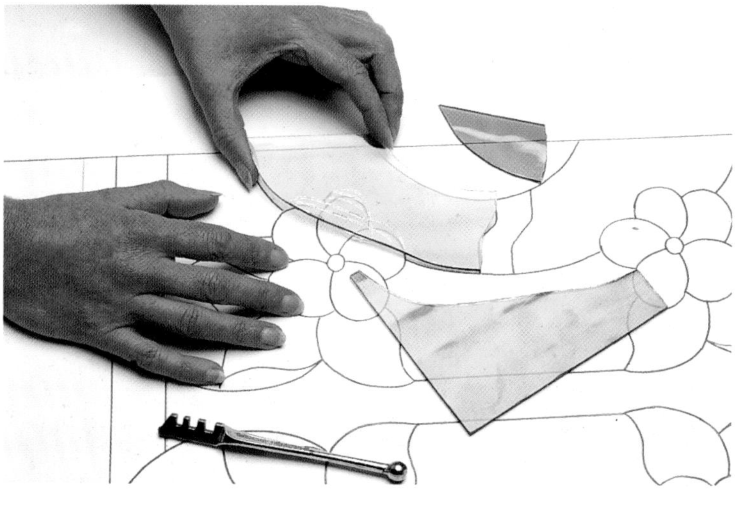

2 Before you attempt to cut any deep curves, first score the main outline. Trim the piece using the pliers. Place the piece back on the pattern and score the deep curves. Now make more scores on the areas of glass you need to remove.

3 Use the grozing pliers and gently, but firmly, 'nip' the glass out, score by score.

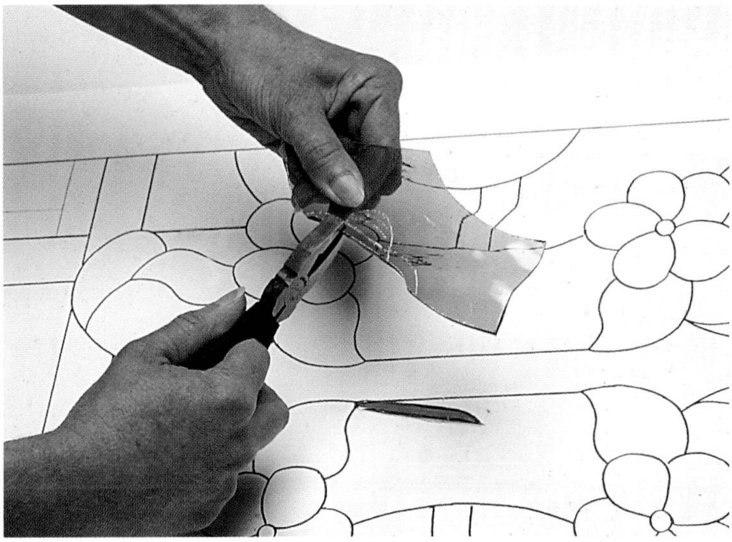

4 Progress deeper into the curve, holding the main piece firmly with your other hand.

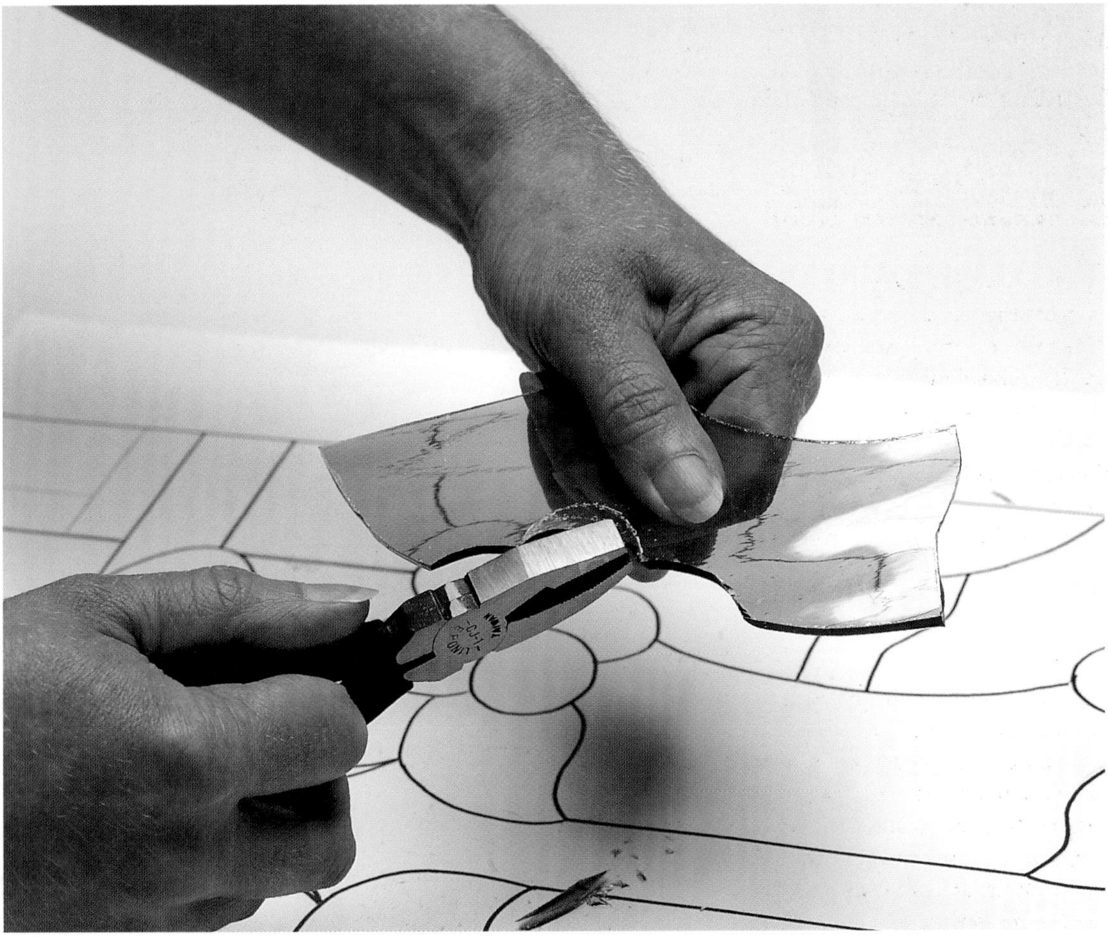

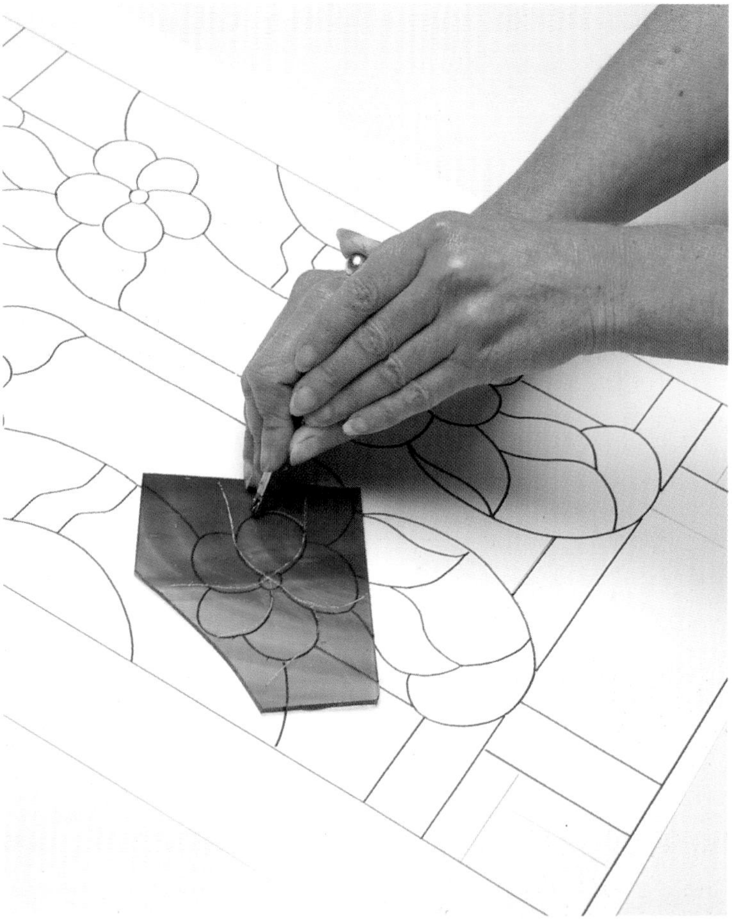

5 Segments of the flower can be cut from one piece of glass. Start your score from one edge of the glass and continue through the centre, following the design line. From this central score radiate the other scores.

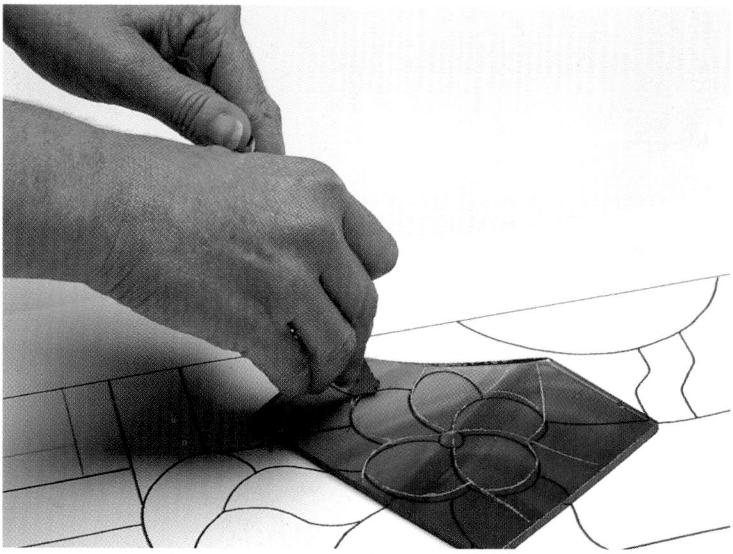

6 Now score the outside lines of the flower segments.

7 Use the ball end of the cutter and tap underneath the scores until the pieces become loose and give way.

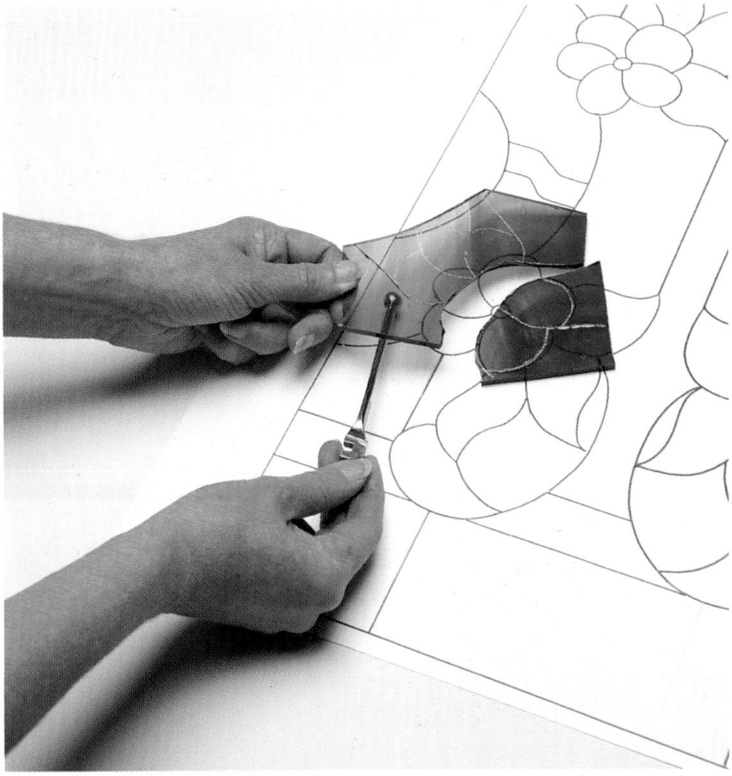

8 Use the pliers to snap off the excess glass. Make more scores for the centre of the flower and trim with the pliers. Instead of cutting very small circles of glass for the flower centres, it is simpler to use small glass gems.

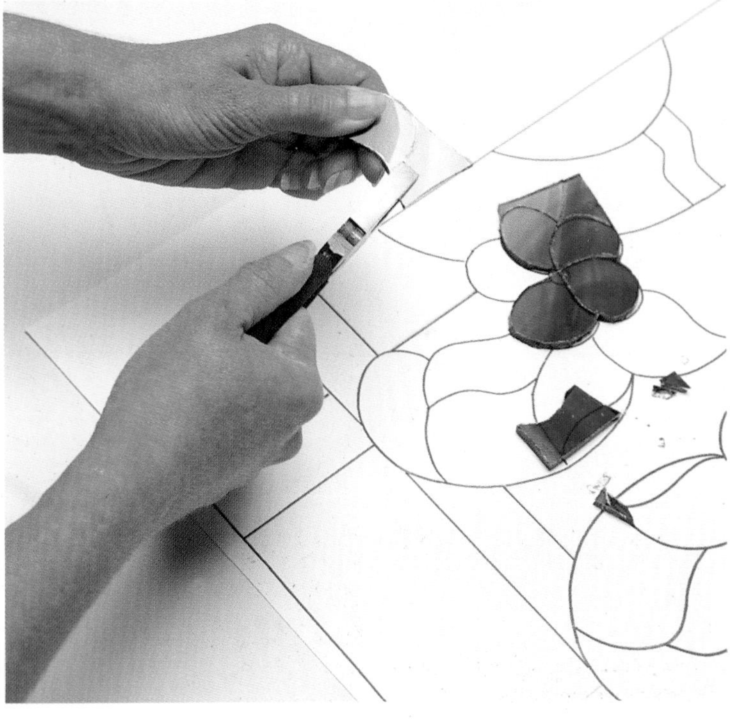

9 After cutting all the pieces, grind to remove sharp edges and improve the final fit. An electric grinder can smooth a rough edge very quickly but can also change the shape of the glass if held against the wheel too long. If you don't have an electric grinder use a carborundum stone.

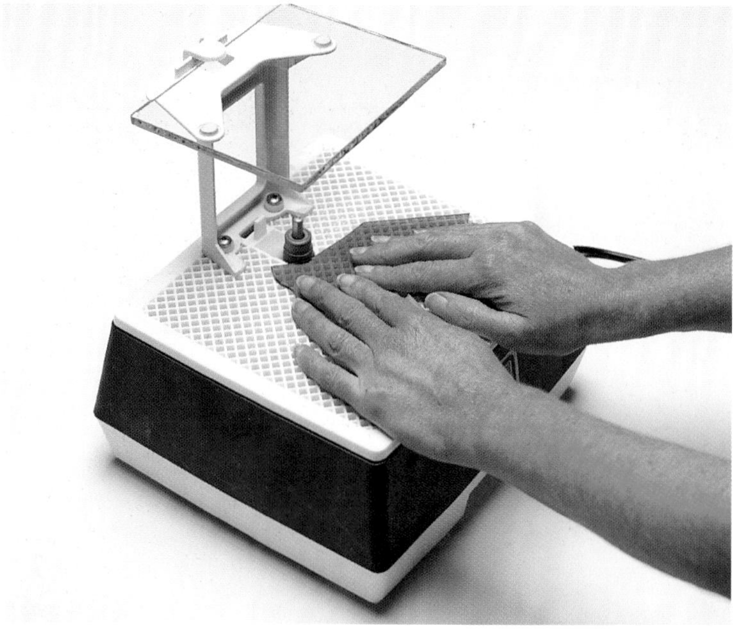

10 Wash and dry all the pieces, then procede to copper foil each one (see page 20 for more details on copper foiling). Lay each piece of foiled glass down on the pattern – a bit like a jigsaw – to form the complete panel.

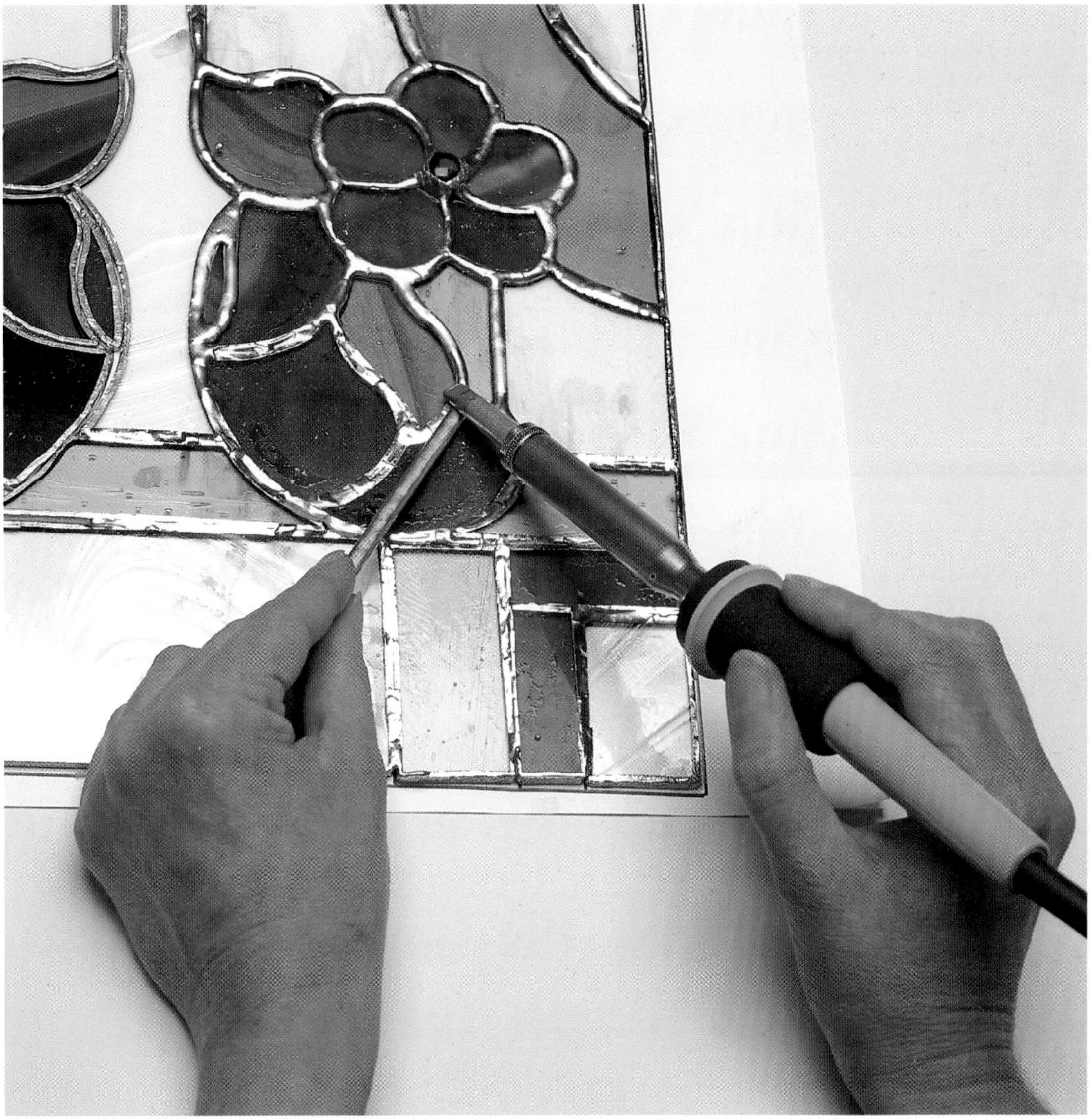

11 When you are happy that the pieces fit snuggly together, start to flux and tack them into place. After tinning the panel on both sides, return to the 'front' and, with a steady hand, bead the tinned seams with more solder. Wash the finished panel and then apply a patina and wash again using hot soapy water.

Glass Gem Mirror

Marc Gerstein

This extremely visual, bright mirror requires a minimum of glass working skills. As with many of the projects, the final selection of colour and design – in this case the placement of the glass gems – is a creative decision that is up to the individual. Before setting the glass permanently in place, try different patterns and colour combinations until you are satisfied with the overall effect.

The background glass is called iridised black opal, a glass with a very 'metallic' appearance that is completely opaque. The gems, or 'flat marbles', are available in a great variety of colours and make an ideal decorative feature.

MATERIALS AND EQUIPMENT

• black iridised glass • 2 mm (⅛ in) silver mirror • large glass gem stones 2.5 cm (1 in) diameter • medium gem stones 12 mm (½ in) diameter • small gem stones 1 cm (⅜ in) diameter • hardboard 35 x 30 cm (14 x 12 in) • brass key mount with screws • wood scrap roughly 5 x 2.5 cm x 12 mm (2 x 1 x ½ in) • clear bath sealant to use as glue • carbide glass cutter • cutting square • ruler • felt tip pen • wet and dry sandpaper, medium grade

1 Cut the background glass first. This piece measures 33 x 28 cm (13 x 11 in) when cut. Measuring with the ruler, line up your cutter next to the straight edge. When using the edge as a cutting guide, pull the cutter towards your body with a steady, even pressure.

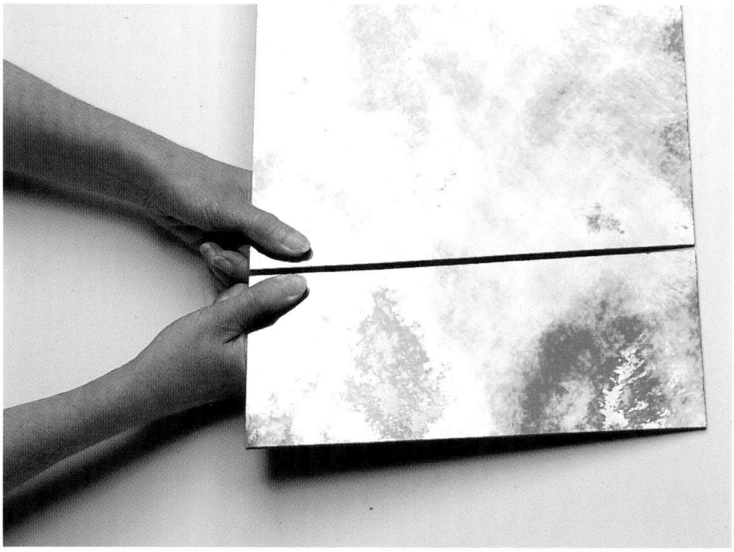

2 To ensure that you have a clean, smooth edge, break the cut using your hands. If the piece is too small to grasp with your hands, use grozing pliers to break off the trim piece. Cut the mirror in the same way, so that the finished piece measures 19 x 23 cm (8 ½ x 10 in).

3 Using the wet and dry paper, dipped in water, polish all the edges of both pieces. If you haven't managed a clean, smooth break, use the glass file and grozer to remove the ragged areas. Wrap the wet and dry paper over a small wooden block to make it easier to use. Keep the paper well soaked with water as you polish the edge. Make sure the edges are completely smooth to the touch before moving on to the next step.

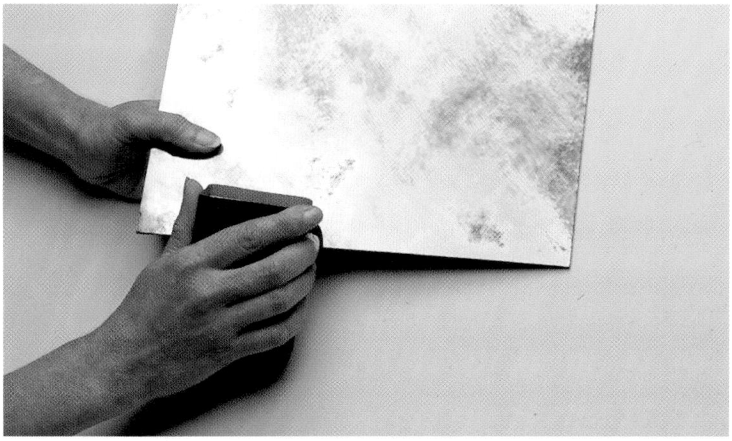

4 Place the mirror and glass gems on the iridised glass and adjust them until you are pleased with the layout. Begin to apply the adhesive, starting with the mirror first, and then working on the gem stones. Excess adhesive that is squeezed out as pressure is applied, can be removed with a razor blade or craft knife when completely dry. When sticking the gem stones, apply the glue sparingly for a neat finish.

5 Screw the metal key mount on to the wood scrap, then glue this whole piece on to the back of the hardboard, towards the top in the centre. Allow the glue to set firmly before gluing the complete backing to the glass.

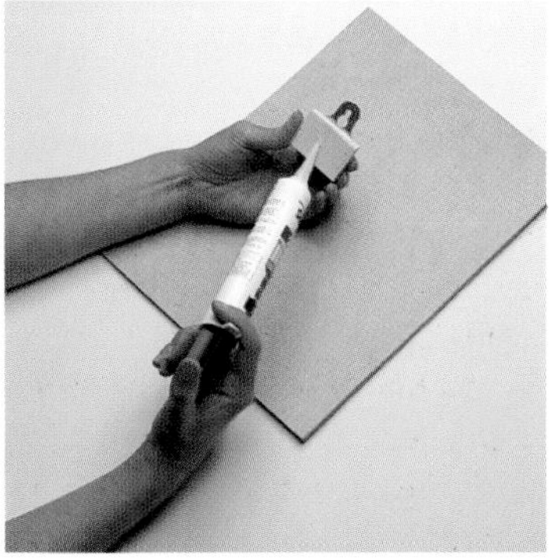

Mondrian Clock

LYNETTE WRIGLEY

Combine contemporary design with a practical clock that will sit comfortably in almost any decor. Moderately priced clock mechanisms are readily available, accurate and one can easily be incorporated into this functional household piece. The bold colours and geometric shapes are reminiscent of the renowned Dutch artist, and the simple, straight cuts make the clock an ideal first project.

~

MATERIALS AND EQUIPMENT

30 cm² (1 sq ft) opal glass in red, yellow, blue, black and white • 7/32 in copper foil tape • battery clock mechanism • solder • patina • paper • felt tip pen • carbide glass cutter • grozing pliers • fid • carborundum stone • soldering iron • scrap wood to make construction guide • flux

......

1 Using the illustration on page 88, draw two full size patterns with a felt tip pen on to two pieces of paper. Take one complete pattern and cut out all the individual pieces. The second pattern will be used for placing the cut pieces on and also as a guide when soldering the project.

2 After drawing the outlines of the individual pieces on to the glass with a felt tip pen, begin cutting. The central red square has a curved section trimmed out at the bottom right hand corner to accommodate the clock mechanism. Cut the first curve.

3 Using the grozing pliers, break the corner piece. Now make another curved score on this small piece and remove it. Place the tiny piece you have left back into the corner. You should now have an oval space left for the clock fitting. Check the opening for size with the fitting of the clock movement before continuing.

4 Smooth any sharp edges with a stone and wash the pieces before applying the copper foil. Ensure the edge of the glass is placed in the centre of the foil. Press the sides of the foil down on to the surfaces and rub with a fid to ensure they have made firm contact with the glass.

5 Use a piece of wood with battens nailed down at right angles as a form or guide. Place the pattern and glass inside the angle. When you are happy that the glass is well positioned and the outside edges are straight, continue to tack solder the pieces in several places.

6 Now solder a bead seam on the front face, before turning over and tinning the other.

7 Position the side pieces and tack and tin together. Slide the base into place in between the side pieces and against the bottom edge of the back of the clock. Tack and tin into position.

8 Place the clock in a horizontal position and bead the seams with solder. Wash the project thoroughly in warm soapy water before applying a patina and washing once again. The clock is now ready to have the movements fitted according to the manufacturer's instructions.

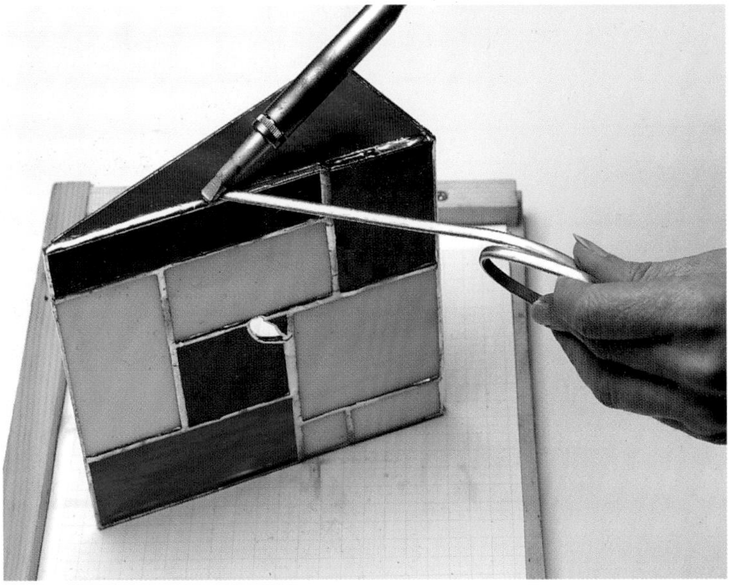

LEADED LIGHT

PETER SMITH

THIS IS THE TECHNIQUE of assembling glass that is generally associated with the great and classic stained glass windows seen throughout the world in churches and cathedrals. The early glass makers had difficulty producing large sections of glass, so formed soft, maleable lead into channels which allowed them to join the small pieces into a larger unit. As glass producing and decorative techniques advanced, the functional leaded light window evolved into the art form we now call stained glass.

The leaded light shown here, makes use of various textured glass that forms a surface pattern, as well as one described by the lead lines.

Take care to position the direction of the patterned glass prior to cutting so that the pieces will not only fit well but also flow together.

~

MATERIALS AND EQUIPMENT

• 1 m² (3 sq ft) assorted patterned glass • 8 cm² (¼ sq ft) coloured glass • 1 x 2 m (6 ft) length 12 mm (½ in) flat H section lead • 2 x 2 m (6 ft) length 5 mm (¼ in) round H section lead • tallow flux • 1 length solder • leaded light cement • whiting • fire grate blackener • cutting square • paper • felt tip pen • carbide glass cutter • grozing pliers • lead fid • lead knife • horseshoe nails • hammer • soldering iron

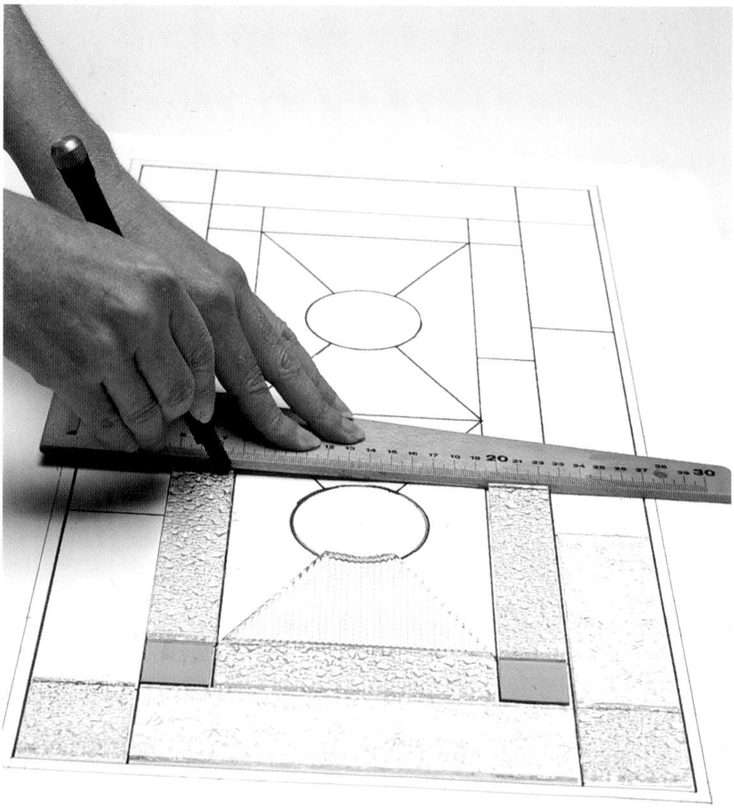

1 Draw out the design with a felt tip pen. It is vital to use a pen with a line thickness of 2 mm (1/16 in). When making leaded panels, an allowance for the thickness of the lead 'heart' must be made when cutting glass. Cut glass on the inside of the 2 mm (1/16 in) pen lines. You will notice in the illustration that there is space between each piece of glass to compensate for the thickness of the heart. This is a very important point! Draw a cut line 5 mm (¼ in) on the inside of the outer edge of your design with a felt tip pen. This is the centre of the 12 mm (½ in) came and will be the cut line.

2 Just prior to use, lead must be stretched, preferably using a lead vice and grozing pliers. Because the cames are relatively soft and pliable, they often become twisted and crimped. Stretching the lead will both strengthen and straighten the channel, making the leading up process possible.

3 Open the came by pulling the fid along the channel.

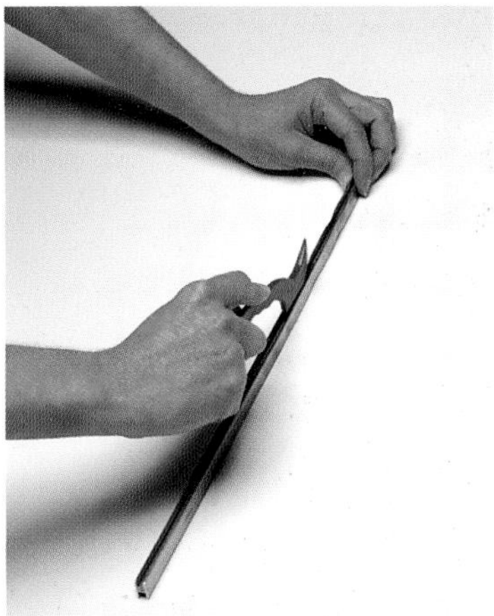

4 Place the pattern on a wooden board and nail down two wooden battens at right angles along the outside lines of your design. Cut two strips of 12 mm (½ in) lead to the appropriate lengths and mitre or butt the ends. Place these against the battens, making sure the two inside ends meet.

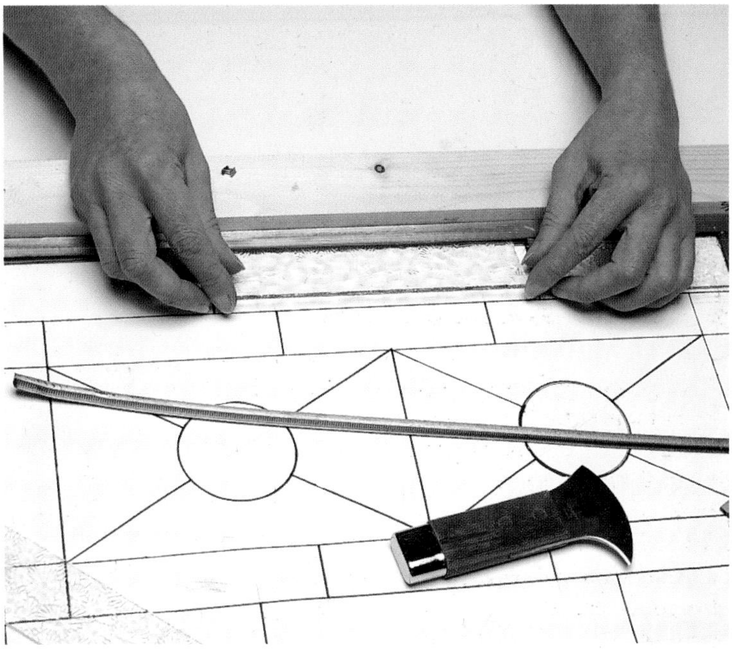

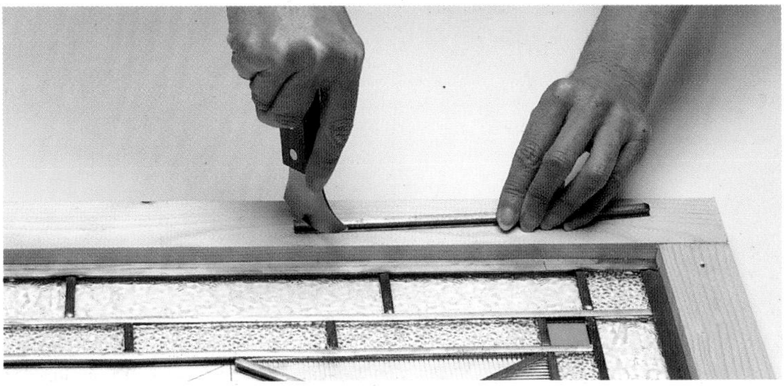

5 Lead is cut by rolling the curved lead knife back and forth across the flat side of the came while pushing downward. If the edges crimp, use the fid to straighten them up.

6 Lead is marked prior to cutting with a nail so that each piece will meet the flange of the adjoining lead. Use a hammer or the weighted end of a lead knife to tap in horseshoe nails into the board in order to keep the glass in position. Use a small piece of scrap lead between the nail and the glass to prevent the glass from chipping. Working from the corner of the right angle outwards, continue placing the lead and glass alternately, always ensuring that the glass is firmly slotted into the came channel.

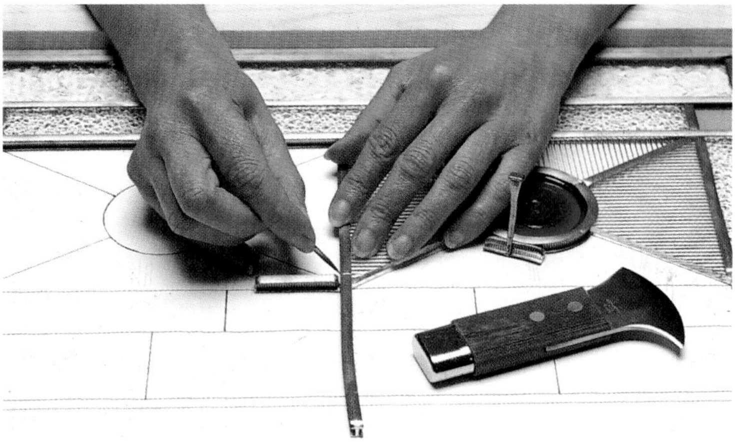

7 When the panel is competely leaded together and firmly held in place with horseshoe nails, begin to rub tallow on to the junctions in preparation for soldering. Small gaps can be packed with slivers of scrap lead. If the lead is oxidized (not clean), rub the joints with a fine wire brush or wire wool before rubbing in tallow flux.

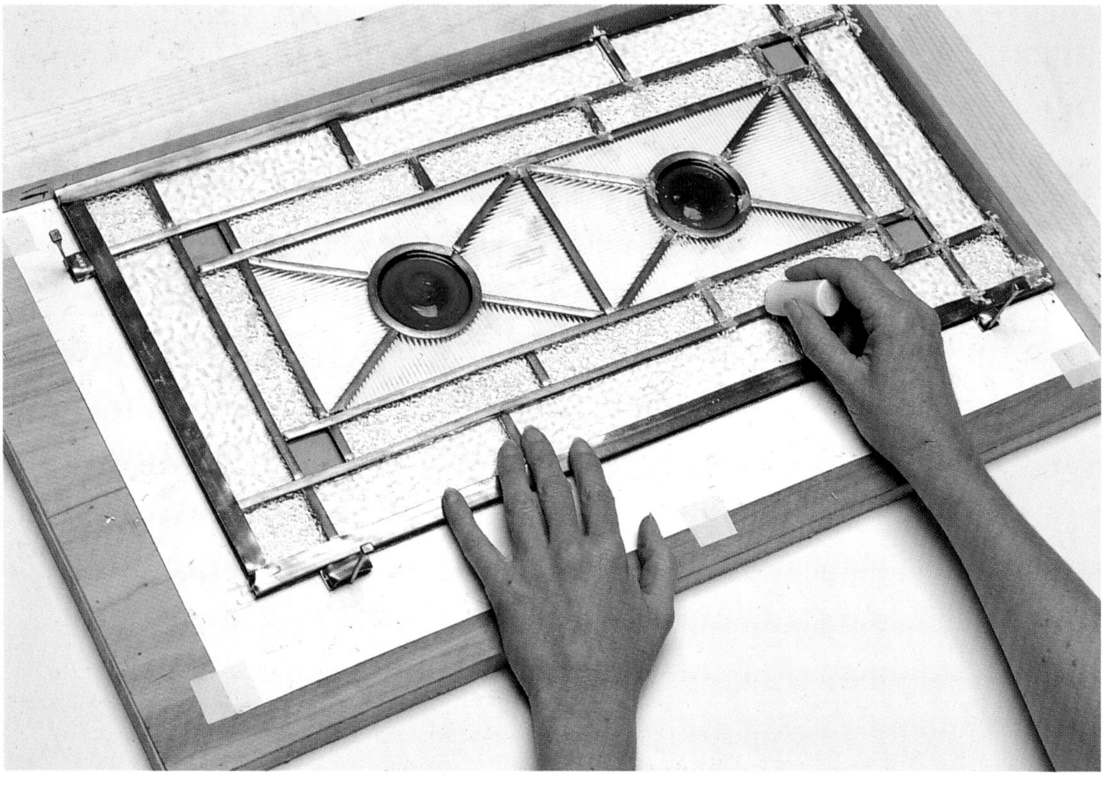

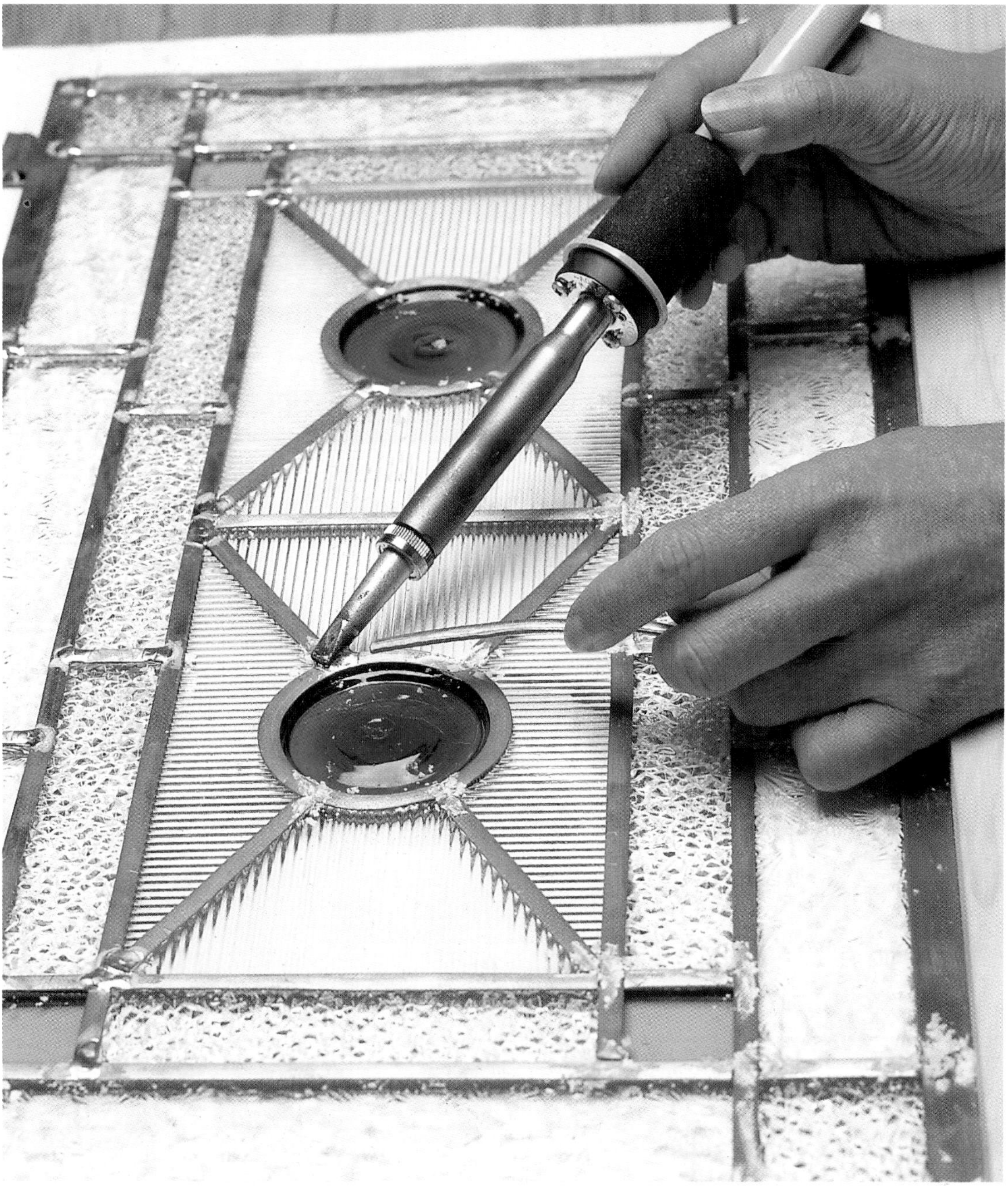

8 Using a hot soldering iron, melt only enough solder at each junction to cover where the lead cames meet. Use the iron with care, remembering that too much heat applied to the junctions can cause the came itself to melt. Solder both sides of the panel at the junctions only.

9 Brush the lead light cement into all the gaps between the cames and the glass. Take special care at junctions. Turn the panel over and repeat the cementing. This process both finishes and weather proofs the panel.

10 Sprinkle the whiting on to the glass and newly-cemented lead. This will absorb the oil from the cementing.

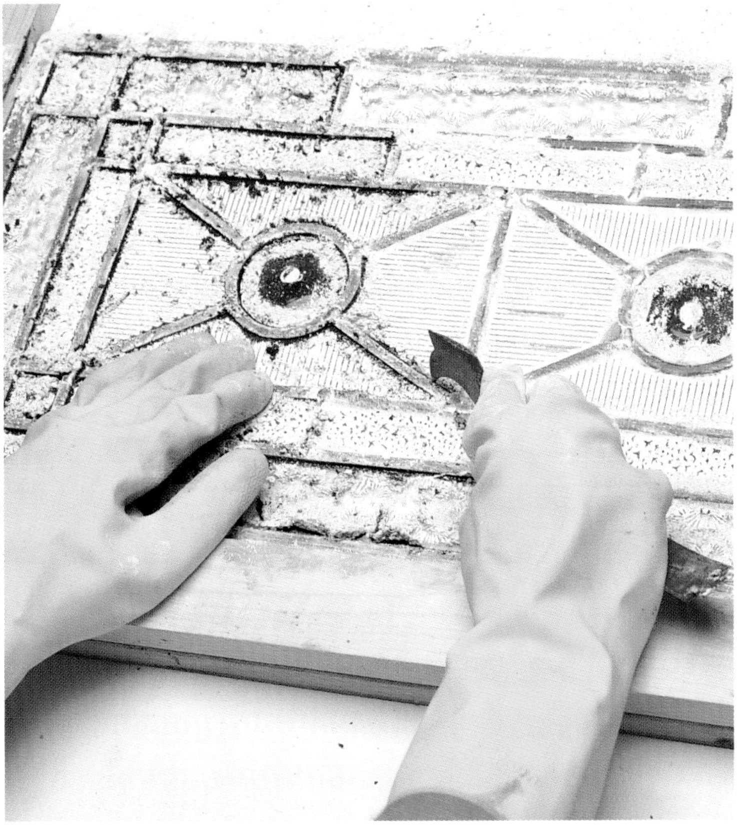

11 Smooth down the leaves of the outside lead and with the fid remove the excess cement. Brush the panel vigorously removing all the cement from the glass and lead.

12 Apply fire grate blackener to the joints and lead lines with a soft cloth; this will darken and polish them. Buff with a soft cloth to finish.

GLASS JEWELLERY

LYNETTE WRIGLEY

GLASS IS AVAILABLE in an incredible array of colours and textures and asks to be utilised in a creative way. Don't think of glass solely to transmit light, but consider other areas where its decorative and unusual qualities can be can be brought into focus.

The jewellery shown here involves cutting simple shapes from a hand-rolled opal glass known as 'fractures and streamers'. This speciality glass is, in itself, an individual piece of art glass consisting of a translucent base overlaid with chips and strands of contrasting colours fused at a high temperature. It is available from stained glass suppliers.

~

MATERIALS AND EQUIPMENT

• *20 x 25 cm (8 x 10 in) hand rolled 'fracture and streamer' opal glass* • *5 mm (¼ in) copper foil tape*
• *solder* • *soldering iron*
• *liquid flux* • *thick paper*
• *felt tip pen* • *scissors*
• *carbide glass cutter*
• *grozing pliers*
• *carborundum stone* • *black leather thong* • *silver jump rings* • *metal beads*
• *necklace clasp* • *earring findings*

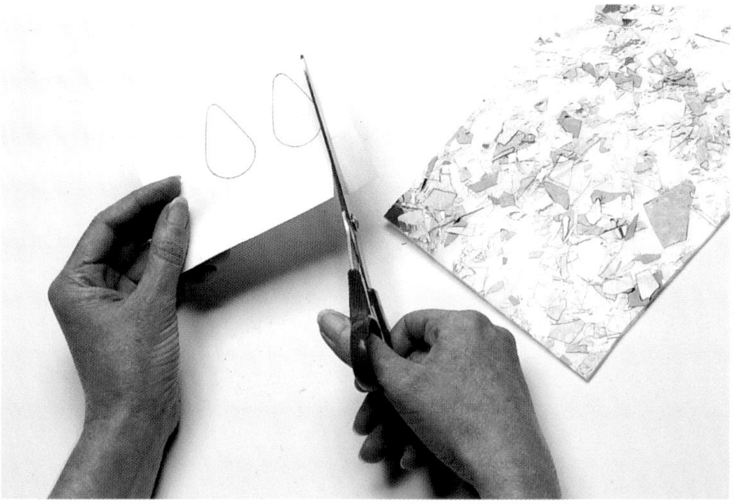

1 Using the photographs as a guide, draw oval and rectangular patterns on to thick paper and cut them out with a pair of scissors.

2 Move the templates around the glass and outline the area of your choice with felt tip pen. As it is difficult to cut glass on the textured side, hold the glass up to the light and re-trace the pattern on the smooth side.

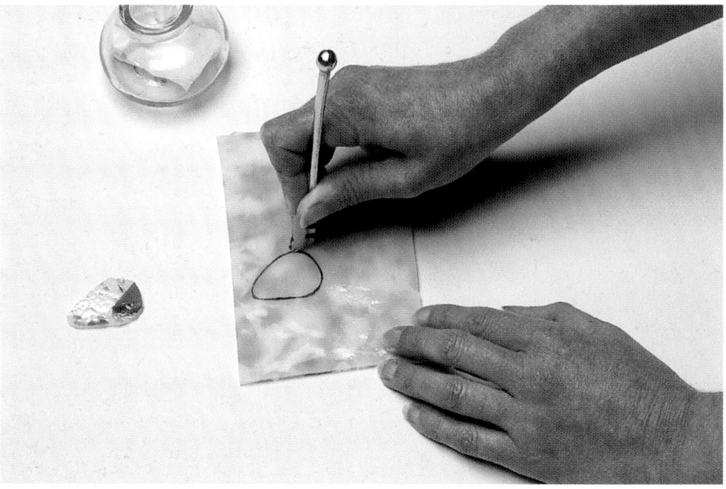

3 Using the glass cutter and grozing pliers begin cutting out each piece on the smooth side. (See page 19 for more details on cutting out small shapes.)

4 Smooth the edges of the glass using a stone. Apply copper foil to each piece as described on page 20.

5 Flux each piece before tin soldering over all the copper foil areas. Solder the jump rings to the tops of the earrings and necklace pieces.

6 For the necklace, thread the glass pieces on to the leather thong, using the metal beads as spacers which will enable the glass to lie flat when worn. Add the clasp at the end of the thong, or simply tie in a knot. For the earrings, attach the jump rings to earring findings, using small pliers to close the rings tightly.

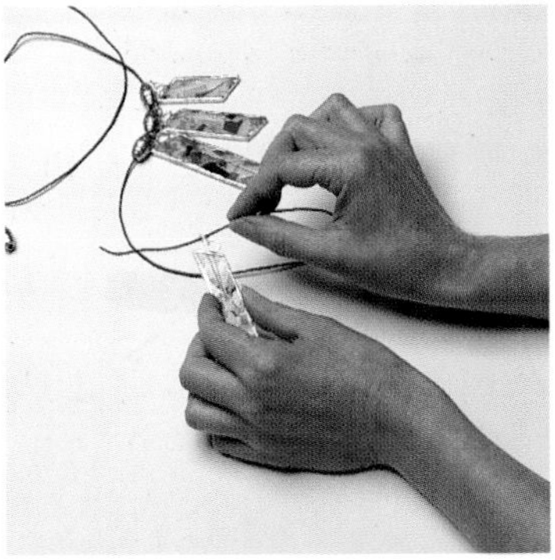

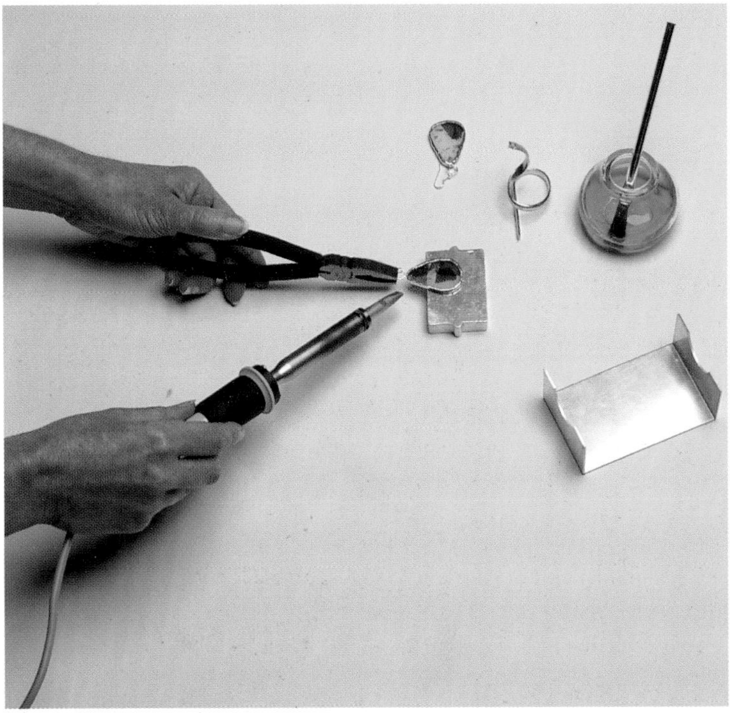

TERRARIUM

RICHARD SCOWEN

GLASS AND ARCHITECTURE have always complemented one another through form and function. Probably the best known effort to combine these two elements was the Crystal Palace constructed in south London in 1851 and completely destroyed by fire in 1936. A building dominated by soaring expanses of glass, the Crystal Palace was an early example of the future use of glass as a key design element in architecture across the world.

This terrarium project takes note of this classic structure through its symmetry and flowing lines. Work slowly and check your work against the pattern as you begin to build your glass plant house. When complete, the terrarium can be filled with gravel and earth to provide a self-contained environment for selected house plants.

Terrariums were originally known as 'Wardian Cases' and were used in the 19th century to transport exotic new plant life from foreign lands on the long sea voyage back to Britain.

MATERIALS AND EQUIPMENT

• 2 m² (6 sq ft) x 3 mm (⅛ in) window glass • 30 cm² (1 sq ft) green opal glass • 30 cm² (1 sq ft) light green semi-antique glass • brass channel • 2.5 x 15 cm (1 x 6 in) tin or brass plate • 2 brass finials (optional) • 5 mm (¼ in) copper foil • 1 kg (2 lb) solder • patina • carbide glass cutter • cutting square • ruler • carborundum stone • tin snips • soldering iron • wet and dry paper • scrap wood to make construction guide • flux

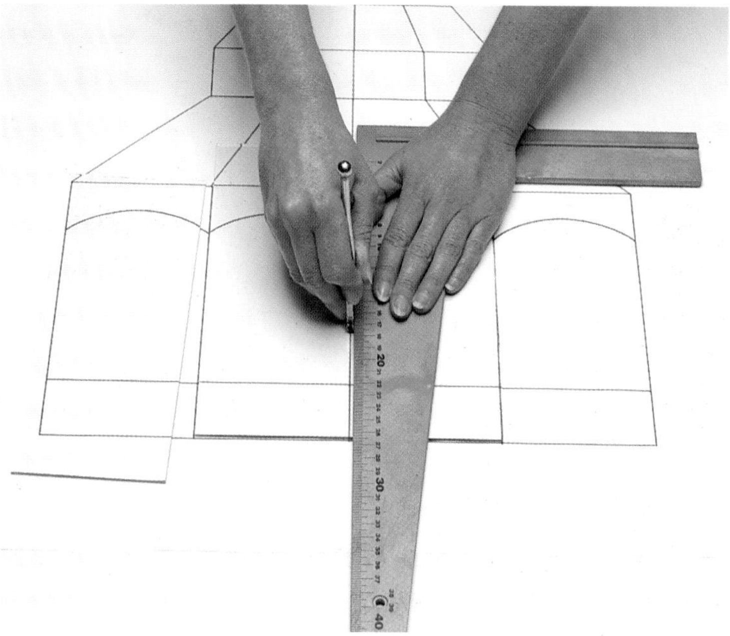

1 Enlarge the pattern on page 87 to size and begin cutting the window glass with the cutting square. You may find it helpful to number each piece within each unit with a felt tip pen as you cut them out. Cut the curved pieces freehand. (Glass cutting on this project is not difficult but must be accurate for correct assembly.) Gently smooth the edges with the stone prior to washing and foiling.

2 Place the cut sections back on the pattern and solder them together into units. Tin the seams on one side and then turn the unit over and solder the other side to form a bead. This side will be the outside of the terrarium. Tin the edges but leave the sides free of solder. Remove one clear piece with a top curve when assembling the second large side section. This will become the opening for the door. The piece that's been removed will become the door. Remove the copper foil on this piece and polish the side with wet and dry paper.

3 Using the door panel piece as a guide, place a length of the brass channel around the glass and mark the corners with a felt tip pen for mitring.

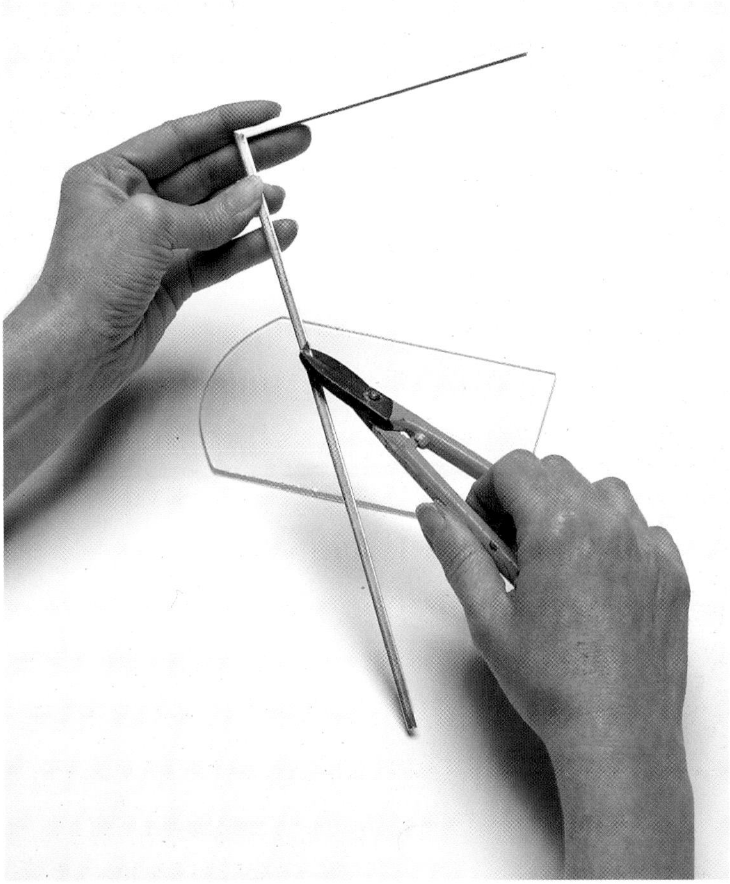

4 Use the tin snips to clip the brass channel to form two 90 degree angles. Trim the ends of the brass.

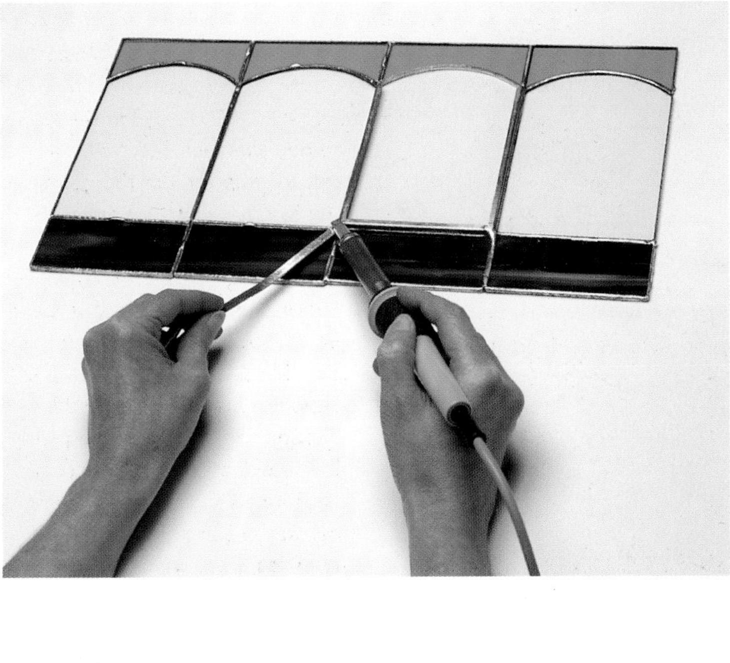

5 Keep the glass door in the brass channel and place the whole piece carefully over the door opening. Tack solder at the corners of the door on to the seams and then solder the brass to the copper along the edges. Now remove the glass door from the brass channel and continue to assemble and solder all the units.

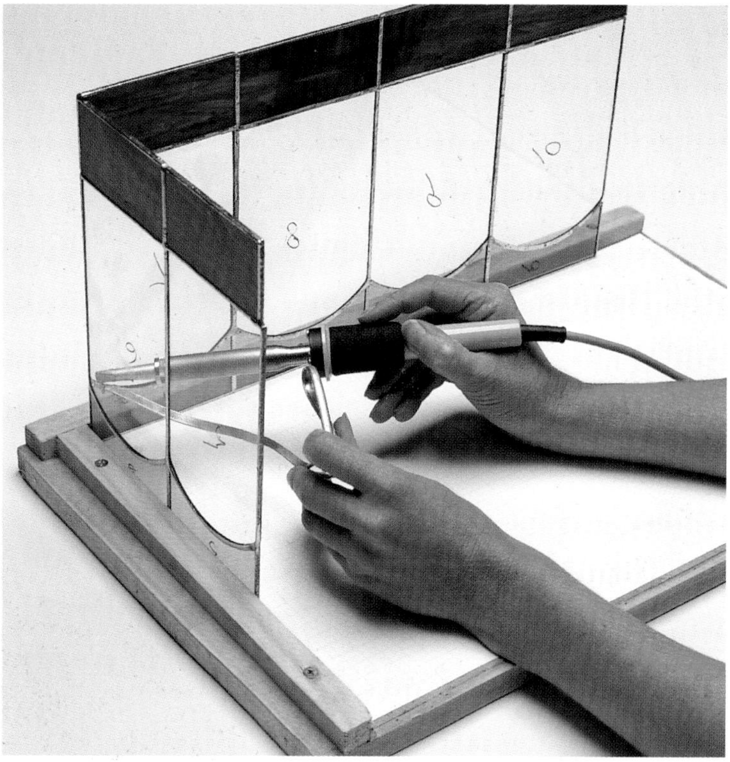

6 Nail two battens on to a piece of wood to form a right angle as a guide for building the terrarium. Place the back and one side unit upside down and edge to edge. Tack on the inside, top and bottom. Repeat the process with the front and other side unit and join the two halves together. Turn the whole unit the right way up, with the opal glass at the bottom. All four walls will now be standing and ready for the upper panels.

7 Position and tack solder the front roof using the vertical lines as a reference point. Tack solder where lines from the lower and roof sections meet. A piece of wood or an assistant can prop this section until it is supported with the next piece.

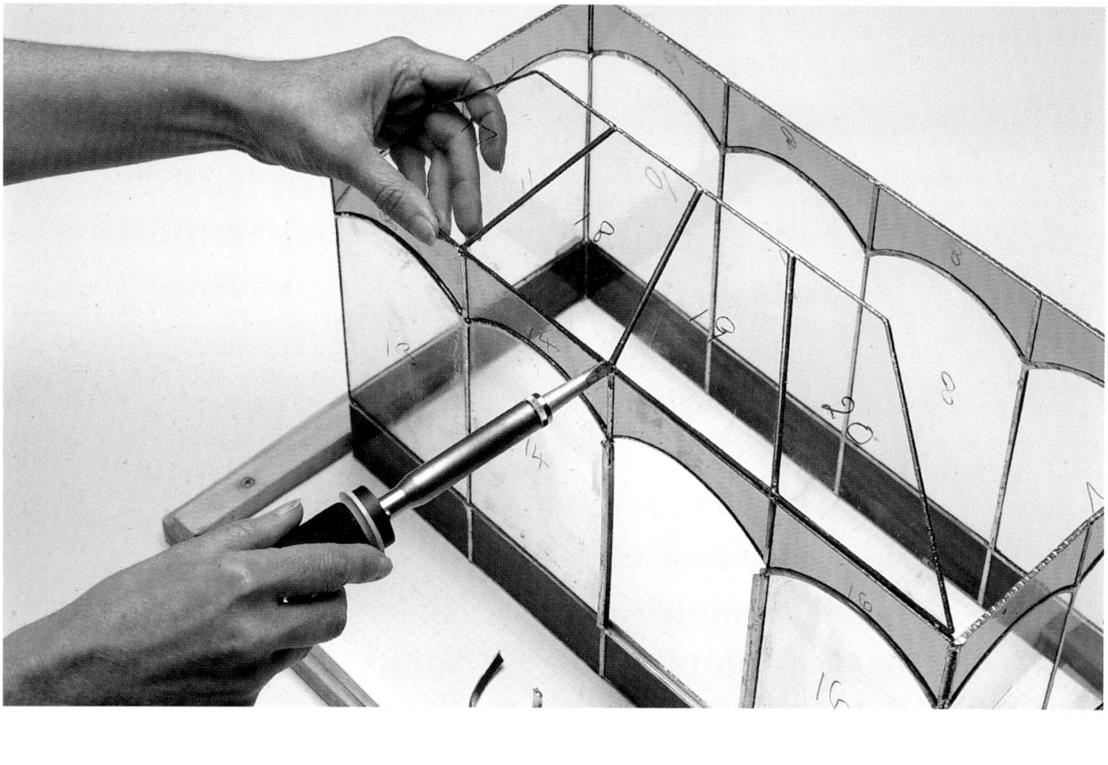

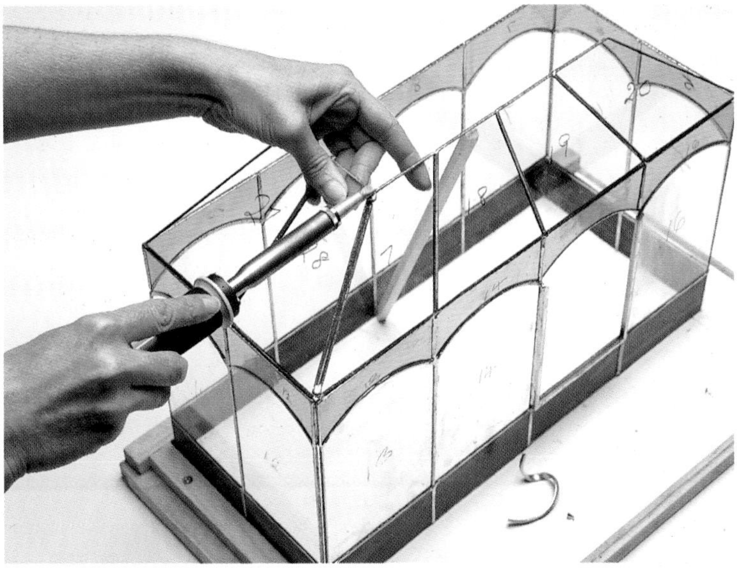

8 Now tack solder the side roof section into position. At this point you will appreciate your attention to accurate cutting earlier! Position and tack solder the remaining roof sections. The four walls with the first roof section will now be standing.

9 Position and tack solder the front and side vertical walls of the upper level. Reach inside with your iron and tack solder.

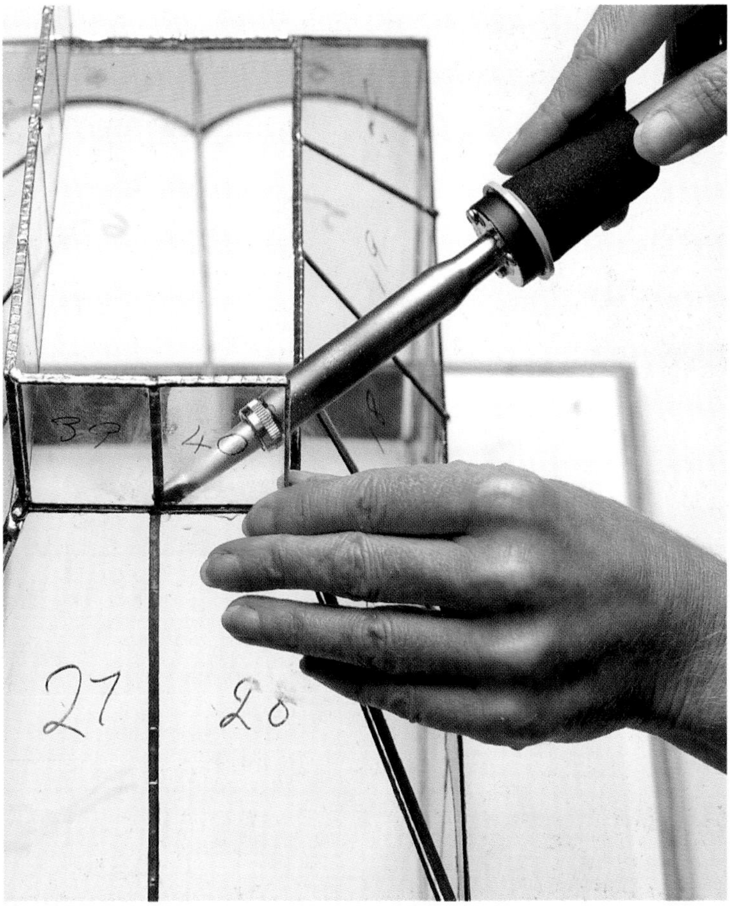

10 Tack solder the upper sections into position.

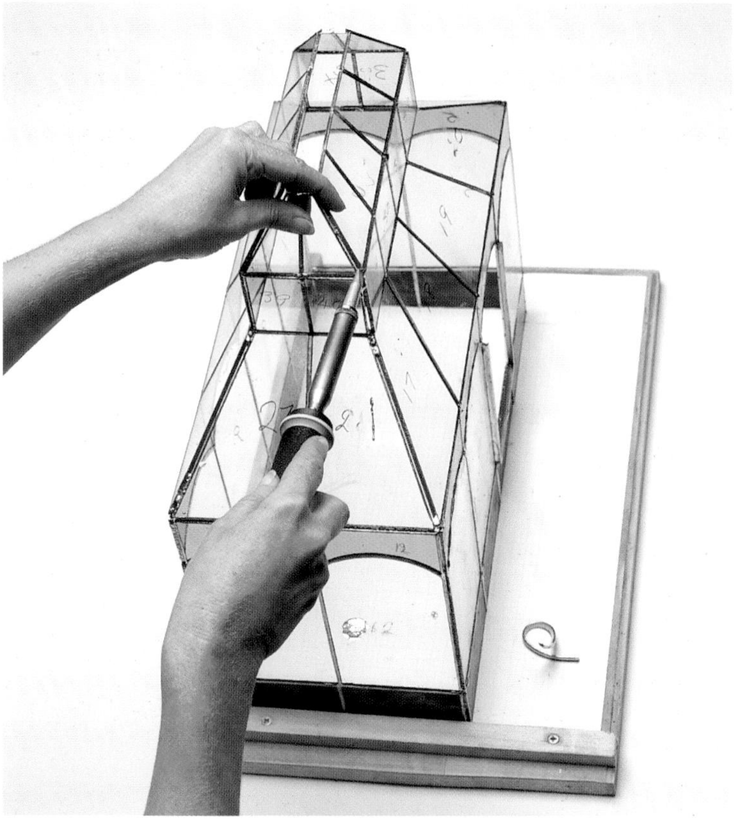

11 Cut some tin or brass plate and solder along the top seam where the metal meets the foil. Now tin the rest of the plate.

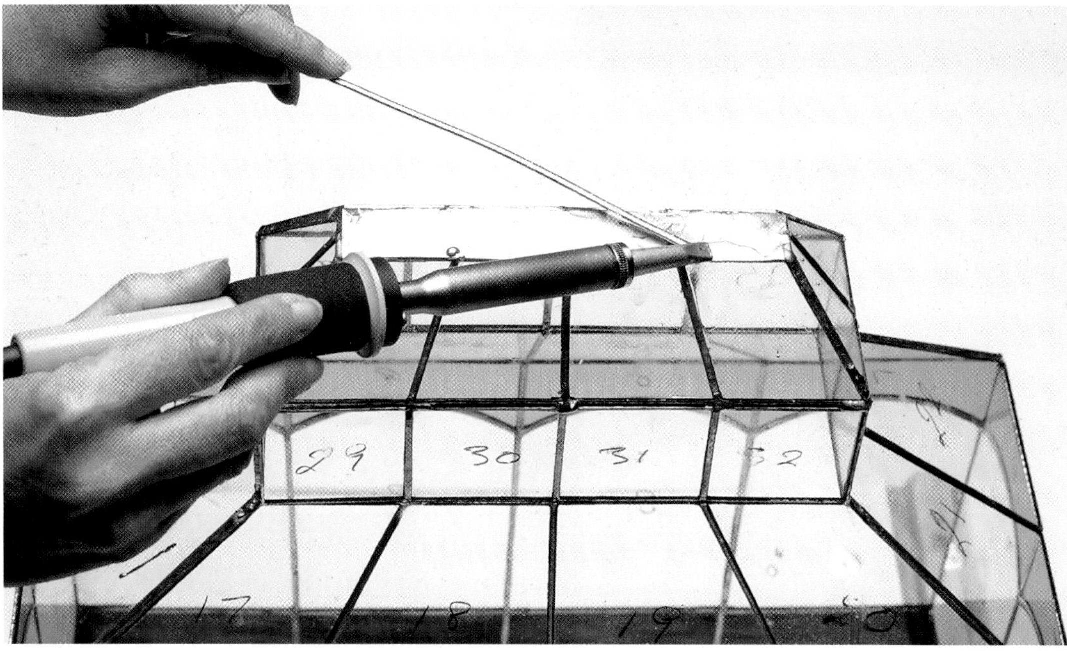

12 Lay the project on its side and begin to fill in the seams with solder, aiming for a smooth beaded finish. You will find it easier to work with the piece lying horizontal when soldering a seam.

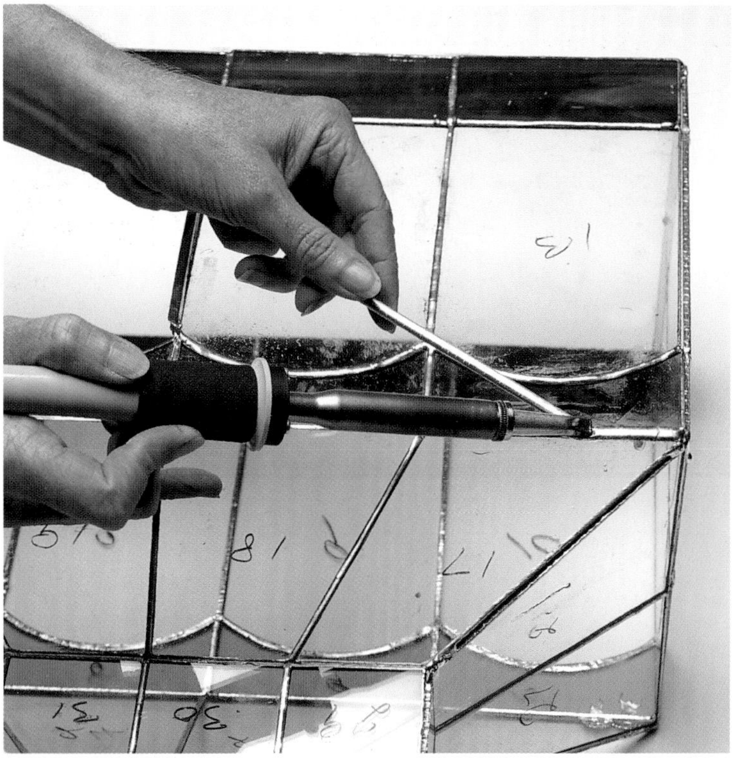

13 Place the terrarium over a piece of glass larger than the entire base and trace around the inside with a felt tip pen. This will ensure that the base fits inside the walls. Cut out the base following the pen line and check for fit before foiling and tin soldering. Then lift the terrarium over the base and solder inside and out.

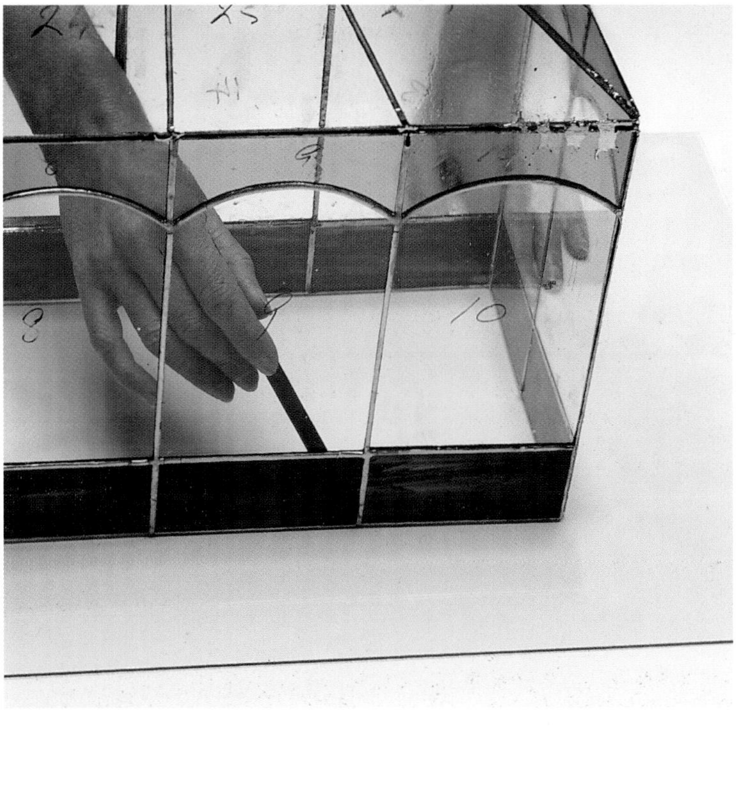

14 For the finishing touch, solder brass finials to the metal top. Complete the terrarium by coating the solder with either copper or black patina and then carefully wash in warm soapy water. The project is complete and ready for planting.

FROSTED VASE

MARC GERSTEIN

AN ORDINARY GLASS cylindrical vase has been transformed into a personalized container as unique as a signature.

Impossible to duplicate, each piece decorated with this technique will reflect the artist's every movement as the 'mask' is applied. Probably more like finger painting, this method of applying wood glue to create a pattern, allows a flexible, spontaneous design. Experiment with the flow of glue using small amounts rapidly applied to create intricate, spider web like patterns. Be tempted to investigate and practise with other materials which could be used as a mask to create different effects. With the mask in place, etching cream is applied to 'frost' the glass and complete the design.

~

MATERIALS AND EQUIPMENT

• *plain glass vase* • *woodworking adhesive* • *etching cream* • *white or methylated spirit* • *plastic bowl* • *rubber gloves* • *paintbrush* • *household sponge with one abrasive side*

1 Clean the glass thoroughly with spirit to remove all traces of polish or grease before starting to apply the glue. Squeeze the glue on to the vase with a continuous fluid hand movement. Depending upon the temperature, the glue will set hard in 8–10 hours.

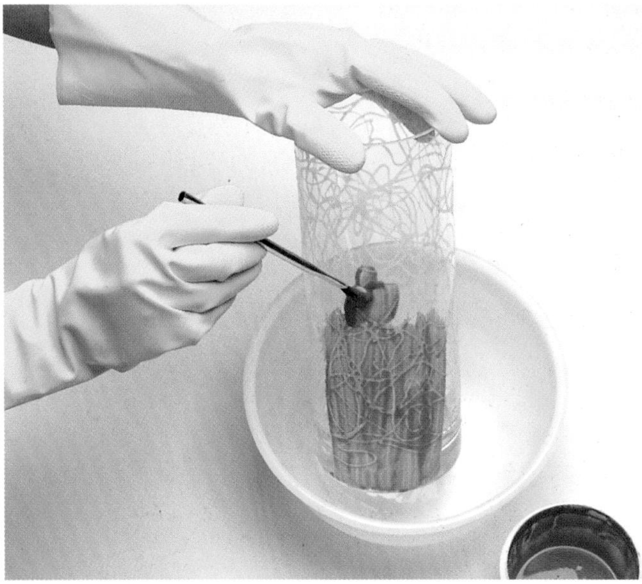

2 Once the glue has set, place the vase in a plastic bowl. Wearing rubber gloves, mix the cream according to the manufacturer's instructions and apply it liberally with a brush over the outside of the vase. To avoid brush marks, apply the cream in a thick, even coat.

3 Allow the glass to stand in the plastic bowl for one hour, then hold it under cold running water and begin washing off the paste with a sponge.

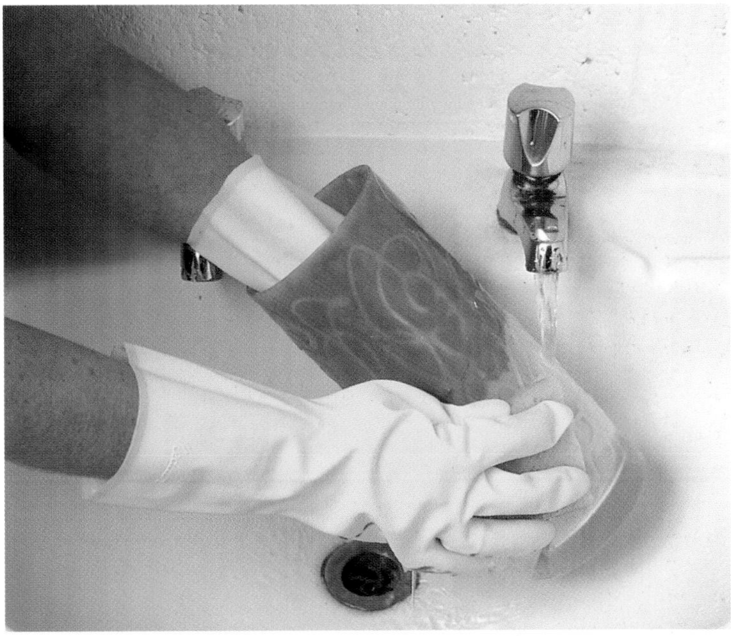

4 Clean the plastic bowl well to remove all traces of etching cream, then fill it with hot water and rub off the glue mask using the abrasive side of the sponge. Wash well and allow to dry.

Candle Holders

Marc Gerstein

Get the feel of working with glass by making a pair of classic candle sconces. This simple project will introduce you to the basic skills, as it requires good cutting, foiling and soldering techniques. Work slowly, checking each stage as you progress from making the templates to cutting the glass in order to develop the skills needed for the more advanced projects. Think about utilising glass in new, unexpected areas where the flexible medium of copper foil allows for creativity and experimentation.

MATERIALS AND EQUIPMENT

- *35 x 20 cm (14 x 8 in) black opal glass* • *2 or 3 mm (⅛ in) mirror* • *5 mm (¼ in) copper foil* • *5 cm (2 in) brass vase cap* • *2.5 cm (1 in) brass strip* • *solder* • *soldering iron* • *liquid flux* • *patina* • *paper* • *felt tip pen* • *carborundum stone* • *pliers* • *wire wool* • *rubber gloves* • *sponge*

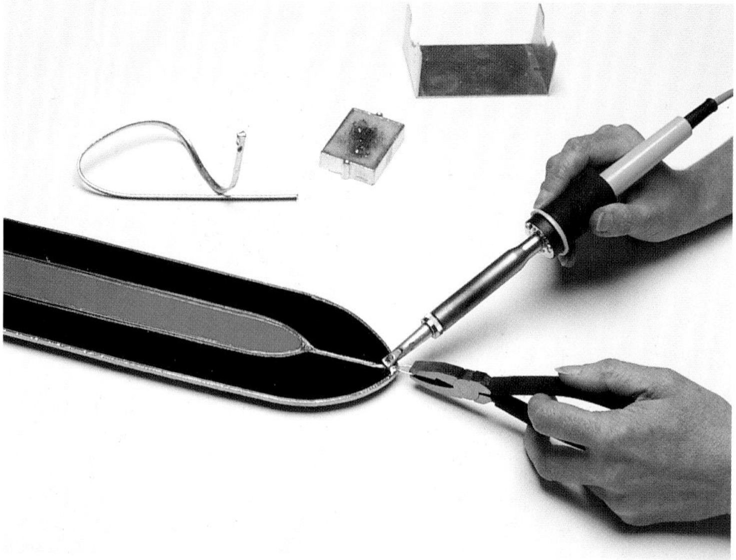

1 Using the patterns on page 88, cut out templates and draw around them on the glass with a felt tip pen. First, cut out the glass for the border and then the mirror. Trim the bottom of the mirror to allow a space for the brass strip which will form the candle holder cup. Check that the brass will fit into the space. Smooth the edges of the glass with a stone and then wash and dry each piece. Copper foil and solder the pieces together, being sure to leave the slot open at the bottom of the mirror.

2 Tin all copper seams (see page 20), building up a slight 'bead' to strengthen the edges. The textured soldering finish of the seams is accomplished by lifting the tip of the iron off the seam frequently, rather than holding it steady for smooth 'beading'. Form a small hanging loop from copper wire and solder in the seam on the back.

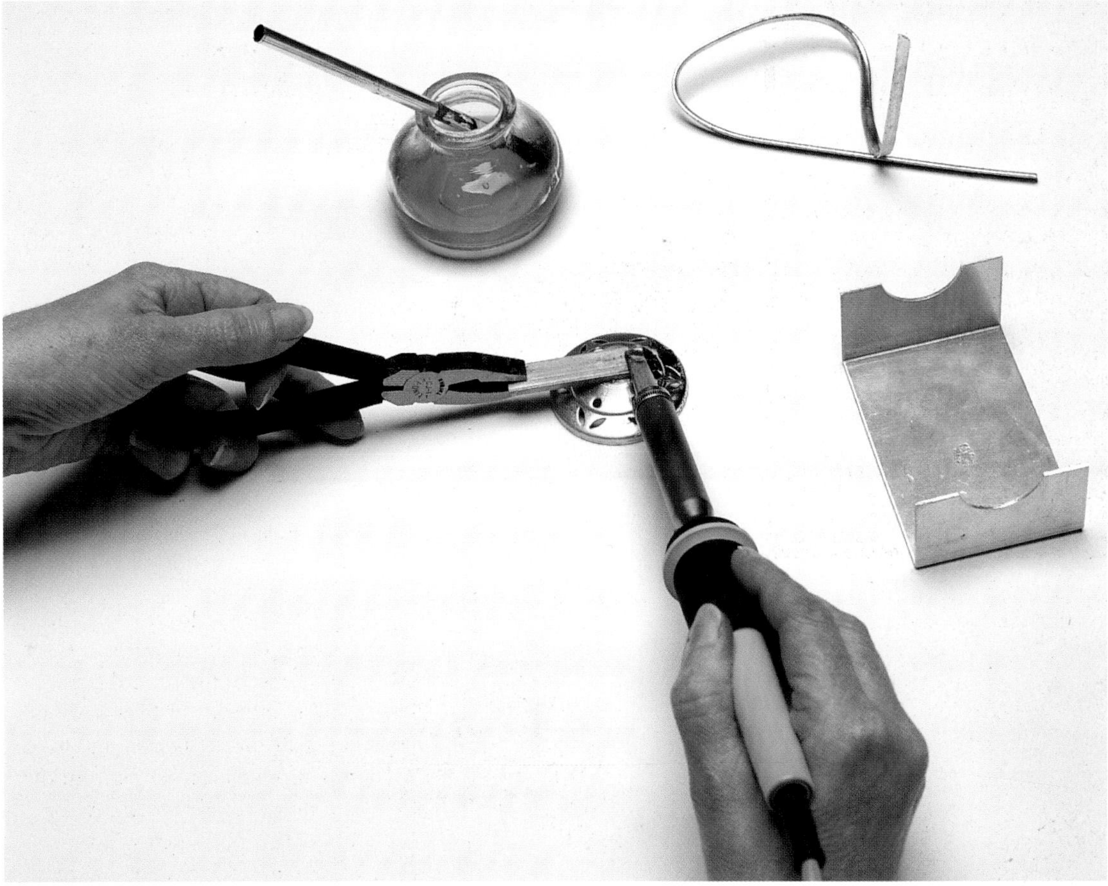

3 Rub down the vase cap and brass strip with wire wool. Using pliers, put the brass strip on the centre of the cap and flux and solder the pieces together. Now lightly tin the brass and cap with solder. This will become the cup for the candle.

4 Place the candle holder cup into the centre of the 'slot' and flux and solder into place. Fill in the areas on both sides with more solder. Wash away the grease and flux with hot soapy water. Wearing gloves, apply the black patina with a sponge and, once again, wash thoroughly.

PATTERNS

Use a photocopier to enlarge these patterns by 200%

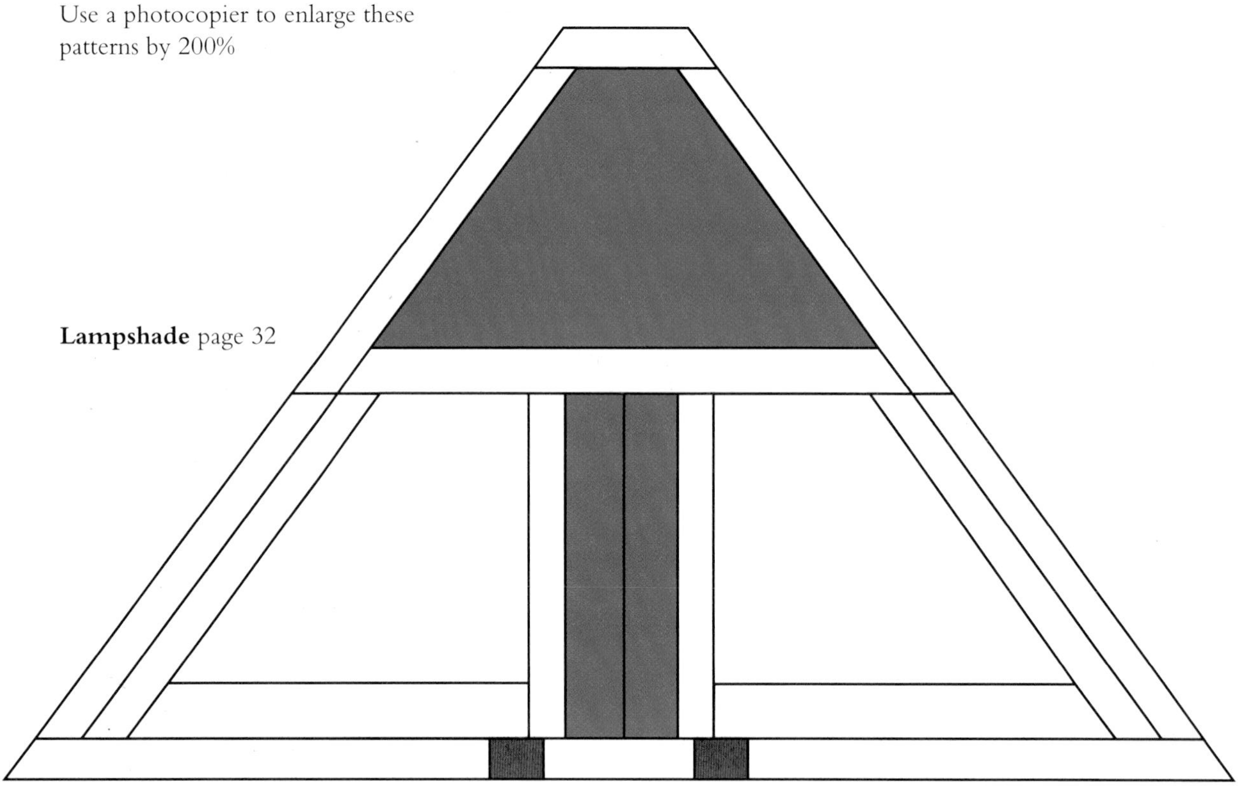

Lampshade page 32

Window Panel page 40

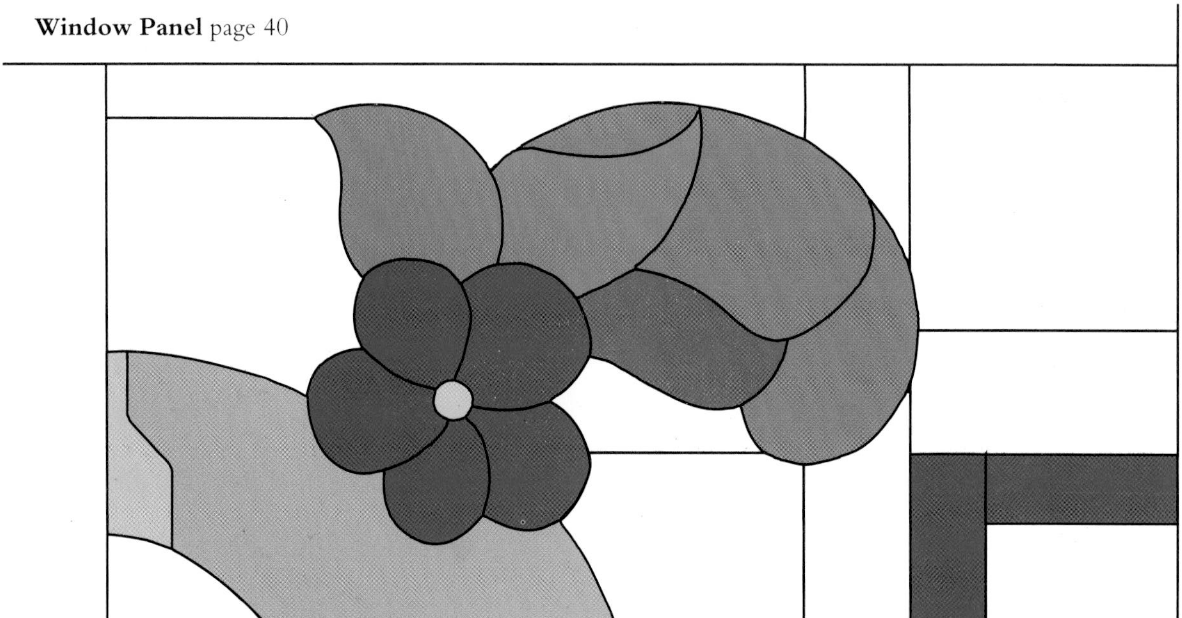

Use a photocopier to enlarge these patterns by 280%

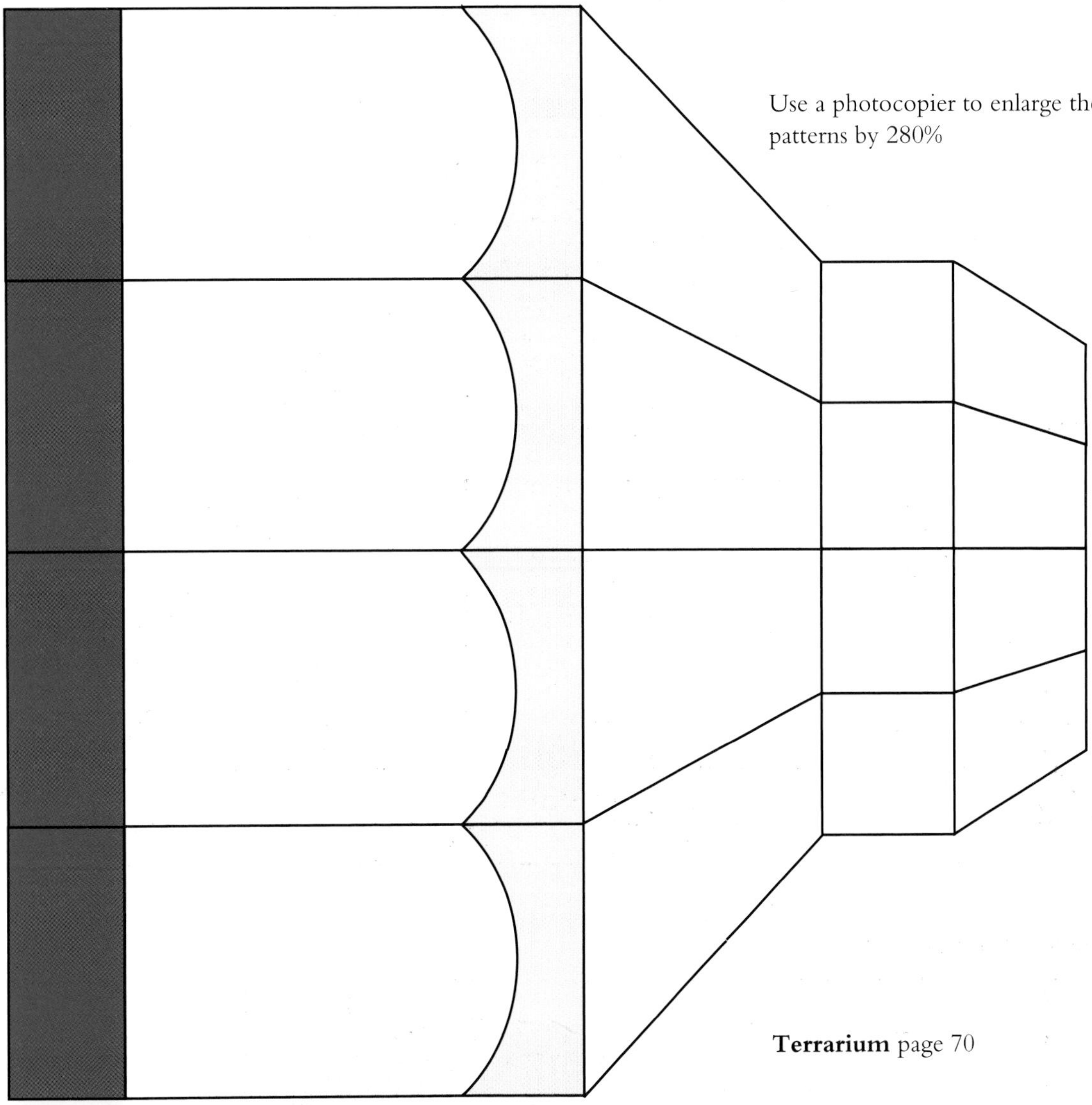

Terrarium page 70

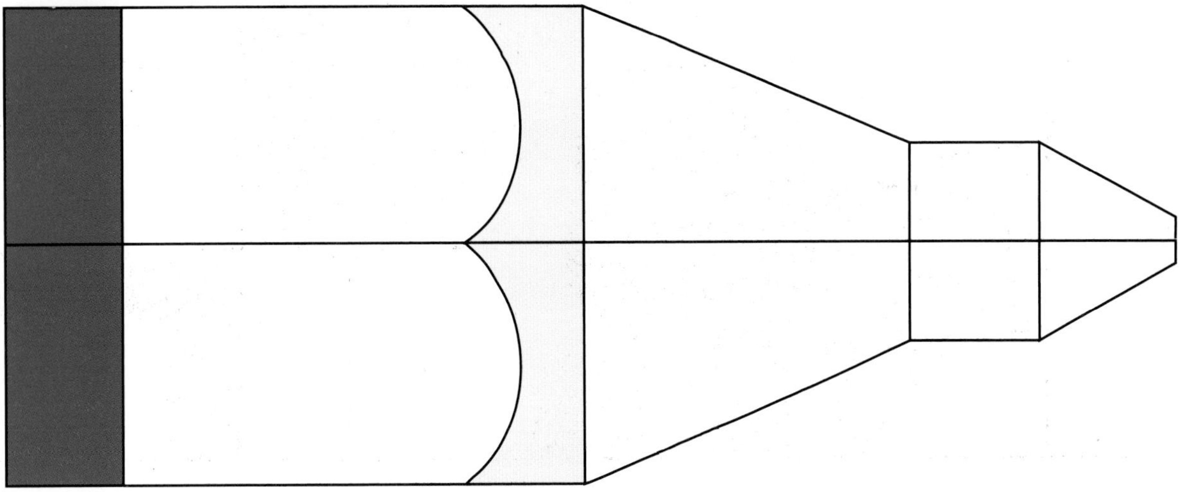

Use a photocopier to enlarge these patterns by 200%

Mondrian Clock page 52

Candle Holders page 82

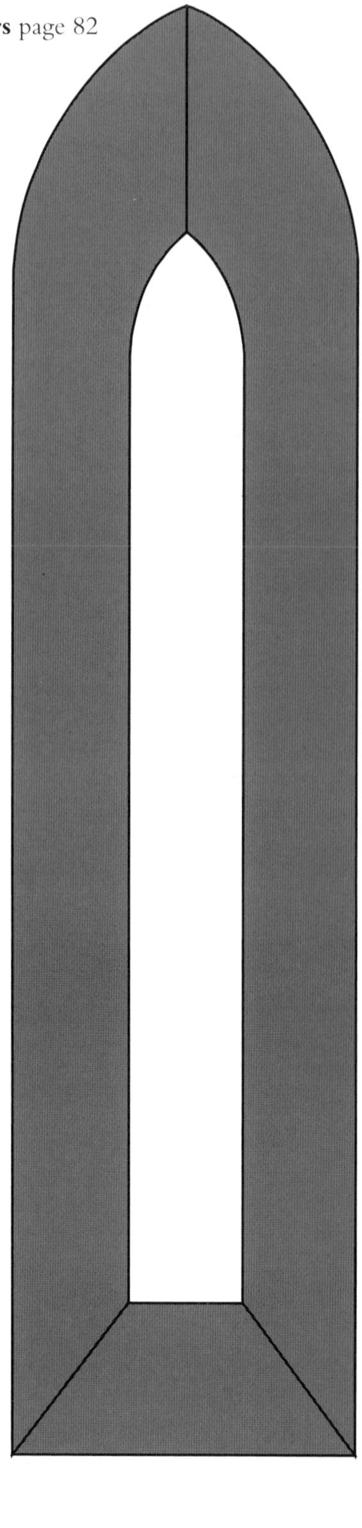

SUPPLIERS

UNITED KINGDOM

KANSA CRAFT,
The Old Flour Mill,
Wath Road, Elsecar, Barnsley,
S Yorks S74 8HW.
Tel: 01226 747424

LEAD & LIGHT,
35a Hartland Road,
London NW1 4DB.
Tel: 0171 485 0997

TEMPSFORD STAINED GLASS,
The Old School, Tempsford,
Sandy, Beds.
Tel: 01767 640235

USA

HOLLANDER GLASS EAST INC,
140 58th Street, Brooklyn,
NY 11220.
Tel: 718 439 6111

ED HOY'S STAINED GLASS,
999 East Chicago Avenue, Naperville,
Ill 60540.

STUDIO DESIGN,
1761 R 34 So., Wall,
NJ 07727.
Tel: 908 681 6003

AUSTRALIA

AUSTRALIAN STAINED GLASS PTY LTD
39 Pyrmont Street, Pyrmont
NSW 2009.
Tel: 02 660 7424/7444

THE STAINED GLASS SHOPPE,
129 Boundary Road, Peakhurst
NSW 2210.
Tel: 02 533 4333

THE AUSGLASS ASSOCIATION,
PO Box 8089,
Hindley Street, Adelaide,
South Australia 5000
Tel: 08 364 3170

FITZROY STAINED GLASS,
392 Queen's Parade,
North Fitzroy,
Victoria 3068.
Tel: 03 482 3622

THE STAINED GLASS CENTRE,
221 Hale Street,
Petrie Terrace,
Queensland 4000.
Tel: 07 369 0914

NEW ZEALAND

A TOUCH OF GLASS,
670 Mt Albert Road, Royal Oak,
Auckland.
Tel: 625 9466

A BECKETT GLASS,
4/38 Jutland Road, Takapuna,
Auckland.
Tel: 09 486 6836

CHEVALIER LEADLIGHT COMPANY,
130 Kitchener Road, Milford, Auckland.
Tel: 09 489 5671

CLARE STAINED GLASS,
23 Jervois Road, Ponsonby, Auckland.
Tel: 09 360 1997

GLASS EXPRESSIONS,
220 Arthur Street, Onehunga, Auckland.
Tel: 09 636 9903

LEADLIGHT WORLD,
12 Beaconsfield Road, Grey Lynn, Auckland.
Tel: 09 376 4793

SOUTH AFRICA

GLASS ROOTS,
226 Long Street, Cape Town.
Tel: (021) 23 0552
Fax: (021) 557 3789

META MANUFACTURING,
305 Umbilo Road, Durban.
Tel: (031) 305 3307
Fax: (031) 305 3321

THE CRAFTSMAN,
Shop 10, Progress House,
110 Bordeaux Drive, Randburg.
Tel: (011) 787 1846
Fax: (011) 886 0441

INDEX